EVOLUTION OF SELF-CONSCIOUSNESS

Chauncey Wright

Evolution of Self-Consciousness

By Chauncey Wright (1873)

It has come to be understood, and very generally allowed, that the conception of the origin of man as an animal race, as well as the origin of individual men within it, in accordance with the continuity of organic development maintained in the theory of evolution, does not involve any very Serious difficulties, or difficulties so great as are presented by any other hypothesis of this origin, not excepting that of "special creation "; -- if that can be properly called a hypothesis, which is, in fact, a resumption of all the difficulties of natural explanation, assuming them to be insuperable and summarizing them under a single positive name. Yet in this evolution, the birth of self-consciousness is still thought by many to be a step not following from antecedent conditions in "nature," except in an incidental manner, or in so far only as "natural" antecedents have prepared the way for the "supernatural" advent of the self-conscious soul.

Independently of the form of expression, and of the false sentiment which is the motive of the antithesis in this familiar conception, or independently of its mystical interest, which has given to the words "natural" and "supernatural" their commonly accepted meanings, there is a foundation of scientific truth in the conception. For the word "evolution" conveys a false impression to the imagination, not really intended in the scientific use of it. It misleads by suggesting a continuity in the *kinds* of powers and functions in living beings, that is, by suggesting transition by insensible steps from one *kind* to another, as well as in the *degrees* of their importance and exercise at different stages of development. The truth is, on the contrary, that according to the theory of evolution, new uses of old [p. 200] powers arise discontinuously both in the bodily and mental natures of the animal, and in its individual developments, as well as in the development of its race, although, at their rise, these uses are small and of the smallest importance to life. They seem merged in the powers to which they are incident, and seem also merged in the special purposes or functions in which, however, they really have no part, and which are no parts of them. Their services or functions in life, though realized only incidentally at first, and in the feeblest degree, are just as distinct as they afterwards come to appear in their fullest development. The new uses are related to older powers only as *accidents,* so far as the special services of the older powers are concerned, although, from the more general point of view of natural law, their relations to older uses have not the character of accidents, since these relations are, for the most part, determined by universal properties and laws, which are not specially related to the needs and conditions of living beings. Thus the uses of limbs for swimming, crawling, walking, leaping, climbing, and flying are distinct uses, and are related to each other only through the general mechanical principles of locomotion, through which some one use, in its first exercise, may be incident to some other, though, in its full exercise and perfection of special service, it is independent of the other, or has only a common dependence with the other or more general conditions.

Many mental as well as bodily powers thus have mixed natures, or independent uses; as, for example, the powers of the voice to call and allure, to warn and repel, and its uses in music and language; or the numerous uses of the human hand in services of strength and dexterity. And, on the contrary, the same uses are, in some cases, realized by independent organs as, for example, respiration in water and in the air by gills and lungs, or flight by means of fins, feathers, and webs. The appearance of a really new power in *nature* (using this word in the wide meaning attached to it in science), the power of flight in the first birds, for example, is only involved potentially in previous phenomena. In the same way, no act of self-consciousness, however elementary, may have been realized before man's first self-conscious act in the animal· world; yet the act [p. 201] may have been involved potentially in pre-existing powers or causes. The derivation of this power, supposing it to have been observed by a finite angelic (not animal) intelligence, could not have been foreseen to be involved in the mental causes, on the conjunction of which it might, nevertheless, have been seen to depend. The angelic observation would have been a purely empirical one. The possibility of a subsequent analysis of these causes by the self-conscious animal himself, which would afford an explanation of their agency, by referring it to a rational combination of simpler elements in them, would not alter the case to the angelic intelligence, just as a rational explanation of flight could not be reached by such an intelligence as a consequence of known mechanical laws; since these laws are also animal conditions, or rather are more general and material ones, of which our angelic, spherical[1] intelligence is not supposed to have had any experience. Its observation of the conditions of animal flight would thus also be empirical; for an unembodied spirit cannot be supposed to analyze out of its general experiences the mechanical conditions of movement in animal bodies, nor, on the other hand, to be any more able than the mystic appears to be to analyze the conditions of its own intelligence out of its experiences of animal minds.

The forces and laws of molecular physics are similarly related to actual human intelligence. Sub-sensible properties and powers can only be empirically known, though they are "visualized" in the *hypotheses* of molecular movements and forces. Experimental science, as in chemistry, is full of examples of the discovery of new properties or new powers, which, so far as the conditions of their appearance were previously known, did not follow from antecedent conditions, except in an incidental manner,-that is, in a manner *not then foreseen* to be involved in them; and these effects became afterwards predictable from what had become known to be their antecedent conditions only by the empirical laws or rules which inductive experimentation had established. Nevertheless, [p. 202] the phenomena of the physical or chemical laboratory, however new or unprecedented, are very far from having the character of miracles, in the sense of supernatural events. They are still *natural* events; for, to the scientific imagination, *nature* means more than the continuance or actual repetition of the properties and productions involved in the course of ordinary events, or more than the *inheritance* and reappearance of that which appears in consequence of powers which have made it appear before. It means, in general, those kinds of effects which, though they may have appeared but once in the whole history of the world, yet appear dependent on conjunctions of causes which *would always* be followed by them. One experiment is sometimes, in some branches of science, (as a wide induction has found it to be in chemistry, for example,) sufficient to determine such a dependence, though the particular law so determined is a wholly empirical one; and the history of science has examples of such single experiments, or short series of experiments, made on general principles of experimentation, for the purpose of ascertaining empirical facts or laws, qualities, or relations, which are, nevertheless, generalized as universal ones. Certain "physical constants," so called, were so determined, and are applied in scientific inference with the same unhesitating confidence as that inspired by the familiarly exemplified and more elementary "laws of nature," or even by axioms. Scientific research implies the *potential* existence of the natures, classes, or kinds of effects which experiment brings to light through instances, and for which it also determines, in accordance with inductive methods, the previously unknown conditions of their appearance. This research implies the *latent* kinds or natures which mystical research contemplates (erroneously, in some, at least, of its meditations) under the name of "the supernatural."

To make any event or power supernatural in the mystic's regard requires, however, not merely that it shall be isolated and unparalleled in nature, but that it shall have more than an ordinary, or merely scientific, interest to the mystic's or to the *human* mind. The distinctively human or self-conscious interest, or sentiment, of self-consciousness gives an emphasis to [p. 203] the contrast named "natural and supernatural," through which mysticism is led to its speculations or assumptions of correspondingly emphatic contrasts in real existences. For mysticism is a speculation interpreting as matters of fact, or real existences outside of consciousness, impressions which are only determined within it by emphasis of attention or feeling. It is for the purpose of deepening still more, or to the utmost that its interest suggests, the really profound distinction between human and animal consciousness, or for the purpose of' making the distinction *absolute,* of deepening this gulf into an unfathomable and impassable one, that mysticism appears to be moved to its speculations, and has imbued most philosophy and polite learning with its conceptions. Mental philosophy, or metaphysics, has, consequently, come down to us from ancient times least affected by the speculative interests and methods of modern science. Mysticism still reigns over the science of the mind, though its theory in general, or what is common to all theories called mystical, is very vague, and obscure even in the exclusively religious applications of the term. This vagueness has given rise to the more extended use and understanding of the term as it is here employed, which indicates little else than the generally apprehended *motive* of its speculations, or the feelings allied to all its forms of conception. These centre in the feeling of absolute worthiness in self-consciousness, as the source, and at the same time the perfection of existence and power. The naturalist's observations on the minds of men and animals are impertinences of the least possible interest to this sense of worth, very much as the geologist's observations are generally to the speculator who seeks in the earth for hidden mineral treasures.

Mysticism in mental philosophy has apparently gained, so far as it has been materially affected by such observations, a relative external strength, dependent on the real feebleness of the opposition it has generally met with from lovers of animals and from empirical observers and thinkers, in whom generous sympathy with the manifestations of mind in animals and a disposition to do justice to them have been more conspicuous than the qualities of clearness or consistency. For, [p. 204] in the comparisons which they have attempted they have generally sought to break down the *really* well-founded distinctions of human and animal intelligence, and have sought to discredit the theory of them in this way, rather than by substituting for it a rational, scientific account of what is real in them. The ultimate metaphysical mystery which denies all comparison, and pronounces man a paragon in the kinds, as well the degrees, of his mental faculties, is, as a solution, certainly *simpler* whatever other scientific excellence it may lack, than any solution that the difficulties of a true scientific comparison are likely to receive.

It is not in a strictly empirical way that this comparison can be clearly and effectively made, but rather by a critical re-examination of the phenomena of self-consciousness in themselves, with reference to their possible evolution from powers obviously common to all animal intelligences, or with reference to their potential, though not less natural, existence in mental causes, which could not have been known to involve them before their actual manifestation, but may, nevertheless, be found to do so by an analysis of these causes into the more general conditions of mental phenomena. Mystical metaphysics should be met by scientific inquiries on its own ground, that is, dogmatically, or by theory, since it despises the facts of empirical observation, or attributes them to shallowness, misinterpretation, or errors of observation, and contents itself with its strength as a system, and its impregnable self-consistency,   Only an explanation of the phenomena of human consciousness, equally clear and self-consistent with its own, and one which, though not so simple, is yet more in accordance with the facts of a wider induction, could equal it in strength. But this might still be expected as the result of an examination of mental phenomena from the point of view of true science; since many modern sciences afford examples of similar triumphs over equally ancient, simple, and apparently impregnable doctrines. The history of science is full, indeed, of illustrations of the impotence, on one hand, of exceptional and isolated facts against established theory, and of the power, on the other hand, of their organization in new theories to revolutionize [p. 205] beliefs. The physical doctrine of a *plenum,* the doctrine of epicycles and vortices in astronomy, the corpuscular theory of optics, that of cataclysms in geology, and that of special creations in biology, each gave way, not absolutely through its intrinsic weakness, but through the greater success of a rival theory which superseded it. A sketch only is attempted in this essay of some of the results of such an examination into the psychological conditions, or antecedents, of the phenomena of self-consciousness; an examination which does not aim at diminishing, on the one hand, the real contrasts of mental powers in men and animals, nor at avoiding difficulties, on the other, by magnifying them beyond the reach of comparison.

The terms "science" and " scientific" have come, in modem times, to have so wide a range of application, and so vague a meaning, that (like many other terms, not only in common speech, but also in philosophy and in various branches of learning, which have come down to us through varying usages) they would oppose great difficulties to any attempts at defining them by *genus* and difference, or otherwise than by enumerating the branches of knowledge and the facts, or relations of the facts, to which usage has affixed them as names. Precision in proper definition being then impossible, it is yet possible to give to these terms so general a meaning as to cover all the knowledge to which they are usually applied, and still to exclude much besides. As the terms thus defined coincide with what I propose to show as the character of the knowledge peculiar to men, or which distinguishes the minds of men from those of other animals, I will begin with this definition. In science and in scientific facts there is implied a conscious purpose of including particular facts under general facts, and the less general under the more general ones. Science, in the modern use of the term, consists, essentially, of a knowledge of things and events either as effects of general causes, or as instances of general classes, rules, or laws; or even as isolated facts of which the class, law, rule, or cause is sought. The conscious purpose of arriving at general facts and at an adequate statement of them in language, or of bringing particular facts under [p. 206] explicit general ones, determines for any knowledge a scientific character.

Many of our knowledges and judgments from experience in practical matters are not so reduced, or sought to be reduced, to explicit principles, or have not a theoretical form, since the major premises, or general principles, of our judgments are not consciously generalized by us in forms of speech. Even matters not strictly practical, or which would be merely theoretical in their bearing on conduct, if reduced to a scientific form, like many of the judgments of common-sense, for example, are not consciously referred by us to explicit principles, though derived, like science, from experience, and even from special kinds of experience, like that of a man of business, or that of a professional adept. We are often led by being conscious of a sign of anything to believe in the existence of the thing itself either past, present, or prospective, without having any distinct and general apprehension of the connection of the sign and thing, or any recognition of the sign under the general character of a sign. Not only are the judgments of common-sense in men, both the inherited and acquired ones, devoid of heads, or major premises (such as "All men are mortal"), in deductive inference, and devoid also of distinctly remembered details of experience in the inferences of induction, but it is highly probable that this is all but exclusively the character of the knowledges and judgments of the lower animals. Language, strictly so called, which some of these animals also have, or signs *purposely used* for communication, is not only required for scientific knowledge, but a second step of generalization is needed, and is made through reflection, by which this use of a sign is itself made an object of attention, and the sign is recognized in its general relations to what it signifies, and to what it has signified in the past, and will signify in the future. It is highly improbable that such a knowledge of knowledge, or such a *re*-cognition, belongs in any considerable, or effective, degree to even the most intelligent of the lower animals, or even to the lowest of the human race. This is what is properly meant by being "rational," or being a "rational animal." It is what I have preferred to call "scientific " knowledge; since the growing vagueness and [p. 207] breadth of application common to all ill-comprehended words (like "Positivism" in recent times) have given to "scientific" the meaning probably attached at first to "rational." This knowledge comes from reflecting on what we know in the common-sense, or semi-instinctive form, or making what we know a field of renewed research, observation, and analysis in the generalization of major premises. The line of distinction between such results of reflection, or between scientific knowledge and the common-sense form of knowledge, is not simply the dividing line between the minds of men and those of other animals; but is that which divides the knowledge produced by outward attention from that which is further produced by reflective attention. The former, throughout a considerable range of the higher intelligent animals, involves veritable judgments of a complex sort. It involves combinations of minor premises leading to conclusions through implicit major premises in the enthymematic reasonings, commonly employed in inferences from signs and likelihoods, as in prognostications of the weather, or in orientations with many animals. This knowledge belongs both to men and to the animals next to men in intelligence, though in unequal degrees.

So far as logicians are correct in regarding an enthymeme as a reasoning, a reasoning, independently of its statement in words; or in regarding as a rational process the passing from such a sign as the human nature of Socrates to the inference that he will die, through the data of experience concerning the mortality of other men,-data which are neither distinctly remembered in detail nor generalized explicitly in the formula, " all men are mortal," but are effective only in making mortality a more or less clearly understood part of the human nature, that is, in making it one of the attributes *suggested* by the name " man," yet not separated from the essential attributes by the contrasts of subject and attributes in real predication, -- so far, I say, as this can be regarded as a reasoning, or a rational process, so far observation shows that the more intelligent dumb animals reason, or are rational. But this involves great vagueness or want of that precision in the use of signs which the antitheses of essential and accidental attributes and that of proper predication [p. 208] secure. There is little, or no, evidence to show that the animals which learn, to some extent, to comprehend human speech have an analytical comprehension of real general propositions, or of propositions in which both subject and predicate are general terms and differ in meaning. A merely verbal general proposition, declaring only the equivalence of two general names, might be comprehended by such minds, if it could be made of sufficient interest to attract their attention. But this is extremely doubtful, and it would not be as a *proposition,* with its contrasts of essential and added elements of conception that it would be comprehended. It would be, in effect, only repeating in succession two general names of the same class of objects. Such minds could, doubtless, comprehend a single class of objects, or an indefinite number of resembling things by several names; that is, several signs of such a class would recall it to their thoughts, or revive a representative image of it; and they would thus be aware of the equivalence of these signs; but they would not attach precision of meaning and different degrees of generality to them, or regard one name as the name or sign of another name; as when we define a triangle to be a rectilinear figure, and a figure of three sides.

Only one degree of generality is, however, essential to inference from signs, or in enthymematic reasoning. Moreover, language in its relation to thought does not consist exclusively of spoken, or written, or imagined words, but of signs in general, and, essentially, of internal images or successions of images, which are the representative imaginations of objects and their relations; imaginations which severally stand for each and all of the particular objects or relations of a *kind.* Such are the visual imaginations called up by spoken or written concrete general names of visible objects, as "dog" or "tree"; which are vague and feeble as images, but effective as notative, directive, or guiding elements in thought. These are the internal signs of things and events, and are instruments of thought in judgment and reasoning, not only with dumb animals but also with men, in whom they are supplemented, rather than supplanted, by names. But being of feeble intensity, and little [p. 209] under the influence of distinct attention or control of the will, compared to actual perceptions and to the voluntary movements of utterance and gesture, their nature has been but dimly understood even by metaphysicians, who are still divided into two schools in logic, -- the conceptualists and the nominalists. The "concepts" of the former are really composed of these vague and feeble notative images, or groups of images, to which clearness and distinctness of attention are given by   their associations with outward (usually vocal) signs. Hence a second degree of observation and generalization upon these images, as objects in reflective thought, cannot be readily realized independently of what would be the results of such observations, namely, their associations with outward signs. Even in the most intelligent dumb animal they are probably so feeble that they cannot be associated with outward signs in such a manner as to make these distinctly appear as substitutes, or signs equivalent to them.

So far as images act in governing trains of thought and reasoning, they act as signs; but, with reference to the more vivid outward signs, they are, in the animal mind, merged in the things signified, like stars in the light of the sun. Hence, language, in its narrower sense, as the instrument of reflective thought, appears to depend directly on the intensity of significant, or representative, images; since the power to attend to these and intensify them still further, at the same time that an equivalent outward sign is an object of attention, would appear to depend solely on the relative intensities of the two states, or on the relations of intensity in perception and imagination, or in original and revived impressions. The direct power of attention to intensify a revived impression in imagination does not appear to be different in kind from the power of attention in perception, or in outward impressions generally. But this direct power would be obviously aided by the indirect action of attention when fixed by an outward sign, provided attention could be directed to both at the same time; as a single glance may comprehend in one field of view the moon or the brighter planets and the sun, since the moon or planet is not hidden like the stars, by the glare of day. [p. 210]

As soon, then, as the progress of animal intelligence through an extension of the range in its powers of memory, or in revived impressions, together with a corresponding increase in the vividness of these impressions, has reached a certain point (a progress in itself useful, and therefore likely to be secured in some part of nature, as one among its numerous grounds of selection, or lines of advantage), it becomes possible for such an intelligence to fix its attention on a vivid outward sign, without losing sight of, or dropping out of distinct attention, an image or revived impression; which latter would only serve in case of its spontaneous revival in imagination, as a sign of the same thing, or the same event. Whether the vivid outward sign be a real object or event, of which the revived image is the counterpart, or whether it be a sign in a stricter meaning of the term, -- that is, some action, figure, or utterance, associated either naturally or artificially with all similar objects or events, and, consequently, with the revived and representative image of them, -- whatever the character of this outward sign may be, provided the representative image, or inward sign, still retains, in distinct consciousness, its power as such, then the outward sign may be consciously recognized as a substitute for the inward one, and a consciousness of simultaneous internal and external suggestion, or significance, might be realized; and the contrast of thoughts and things, at least in their power of suggesting that of which they may be coincident signs, could, for the first time, be perceptible. This would plant the germ of the distinctively human form of self-consciousness.

Previously to such a simultaneous consciousness of movements in imagination and movements in the same direction arising from perception, realized through the comparative vividness of the former, all separate and distinct consciousness of the inward sign would be eclipsed, and attention would pass on to the thought suggested by the outward sign. A similar phenomenon is frequently observed with us in successions of inward suggestions, or trains of thought. The attention often skips intermediate steps in a train, or appears to do so. At least, the memory of steps, which appear essential to its rational coherency,[p. 211] has ceased when we revive the train or repeat it voluntarily. This happens even when only a few moments have elapsed between the train and its repetition. Some writers assert that the omitted steps are immediately forgotten in such cases, on account of their feebleness, -- as we forget immediately the details of a view which we have just seen, and remember only its salient points; while others maintain that the missing steps are absent from consciousness, even in the original and spontaneous movements of the train; or are present only through an unconscious agency, both in the train and its revival. This being a question of memory, reference cannot be made to memory itself for the decision of it. To decide whether a thing is completely forgotten, or has never been experienced, we have no other resource than rational analogy, which, in the present case, appears to favor the theory of oblivion, rather than that of latent mental ties and actions; since oblivion is a *vera causa* sufficient to account for the difference between such revived trains and those in which no steps are missed, or could be rationally supposed to have been present. The theory of "latent mental agency" appears to confound the original spontaneous movement of the train with what appears as its representative in its voluntary revival. This revival, in some cases, really involves new conditions, and is not, therefore, to be rationally interpreted as a precisely true recollection. If repeated often, it will establish direct and strong associations of contiguity between salient steps in the train which were connected at first by feebler· though still conscious steps. The complete obliteration of these is analogous, as I have said, to the loss, in primary forms of memory, of details which are present to consciousness in actual first perceptions.

If, as more frequently happens, the whole train, with all its steps of suggestion, is recalled in the voluntary revival of it (without any sense of missing steps), the feebler intermediate links, that in other cases are obliterated, would correspond to the feebler, though (in the more advanced animal intelligences) comparatively vivid, mental signs which have in them the germ, as I have said, of the human form of self-consciousness.[p. 212] The growth of this consciousness, its development from this germ, is a more direct process than the production of the germ itself, which is only incidental to previous utilities in the power of memory. Thought, henceforward, may be an object to thought in its distinct contrast, as an inward sign, with the outward and more vivid sign of that which they both suggest, or revive from memory. This contrast is heightened if the outward one is more strictly a sign; that is, is not the perception of an object or event, of which the inward and representative image is a counterpart, but is of a different nature, for instance some movement or gesture or vocal utterance, or some graphic sign, associated by contiguity with the object or event, or, more properly, with its representative image. The "concept" so formed is not a thing complete in itself, but is essentially a cause, or step, in mental trains. The outward sign, the image, or inward sign, and the suggested thought, or image, form a train, like a train which might be wholly within the imagination. This train is present, in all its three constituents, to the first, or immediate, consciousness, in all degrees of intelligence; but in the revival of it, in the inferior degrees of intelligence, the middle term is obliterated, as in the trains of thought above considered. The animal has in mind only an image of the sign, previously present in perception, followed now immediately by an image of what was suggested through the obliterated mental image. But the latter in the higher degrees of intelligence, is distinctly recalled as a middle term. In the revival of past trains, which were first produced through outward signs, the dumb animal has no consciousness of there having been present more than one of the two successive signs, which, together with the suggested image, formed the actual train in its first occurrence. The remembered outward sign is now a thought, or image, immediately suggesting or recalling that which was originally suggested by a feebler intermediate step.

In pure imaginations, not arising by actual connections through memory, the two terms are just the same with animals as in real memory; except that they are not felt to be the representatives of a former real connection. The contrast of [p. 213] the real and true with the imaginary and false is, then, the only general one of which such a mind could be aware in the phenomena of thought. The contrast of thought itself with perception, or with the actual outward sign and suggestion of the thought, is realized only by the revival in memory of the feeble connecting link. This effects a contrast not only between what is real and what is merely imaginary, but also between what is out of the mind and what is within it. The minute difference in the force of memory, on which this link in the chain of attention at first depended, was one of immense consequence to man. This feeble link is the dividing region, interval, or cleft between the two more vivid images; one being more vivid as a direct recollection of an actual outward impression, and the other being more vivid, or salient, from the interest or the motives which gave it the prominence of a thought demanding attention; either as a memory of a past object or event of interest, or the image of something in the immediate future. The disappearance altogether of this feeble link would, as I have said, take from the images connected by it all contrast with any pair of steps in a train, except a consciousness of reality in the connection of these images in a previous experience.[2] [p. 214]

To exemplify this somewhat abstruse analysis, let us examine what, according to it, would be the mental movements in a [p. 215] man, let him be a sportsman, -- and a domestic animal, -- let it be his dog, -- on hearing a name, -- let it be the name of some game, as " fox." The general character of the phenomena in both would be the same on the actual first hearing of this word. The word would suggest a mental image of the fox, then its movements of escape from its hunters, and the thought would pass on and dwell, through the absorbing interest of it, on the hunter's movements of pursuit, or pass on even to the capture and destruction of the game. This would, doubtless, recall to the minds of the hunter and his hound one or more real and distinctly remembered incidents of the sort. Now if we suppose this train of thought to be revived (as undoubtedly it is capable of being, both in the man and the dog), it will be the same in the man's mind as on its first production; except that the name "fox" will be thought of as an auditory, or else a vocal image, instead of being heard; and the visual image of the fox will be recalled by it with all the succeeding parts of the repeated train. But In the dog, either the auditory image of the name will not be recalled, since the vocal image does not exist in his mind to aid the recall (his voluntary vocal powers not being capable of forming it even in the first instance); or if such an auditory image arises, the representative visual or olfactory[3] one will not appear in distinct consciousness. His attention will pass at once from either of these signs, but from one only to the more intense and interesting parts of the train, -- to the pursuit and capture of the game, or to actually remembered incidents of the kind. Either the first or the immediate sign will remain in oblivion.

Hence the dog's dreams, or trains of thought, when they are revivals of previous trains, or when they rise into prominent consciousness in consequence of having been passed through [p. 216] before, omit or skip over the Steps which at first served only as suggesting and connecting signs, following now only the associations of contiguity, established in the first occurrence of the train between its more prominent parts. The suggested thought eclipses by its glare the suggesting one. The interest of an image, or its power to attract attention and increased force, depends in the dog only on its vividness as a memory, of as a future purpose or event, and very little, if at all, on its relations and agency as a *sign*. Images, as well as outward signs, serve, as I have said, in the dumb animals as well as in man in this capacity; but this is not *recognized* by the animal, since those parts of a train which serve only as signs are too feeble to be revived in the repeated train; and new associations of mere contiguity in the prominent parts of it take their places. All that would be recognized in the animal mind by reflection on thought as thought, or independently of its reality as a memory, an anticipation, or a purpose, would be its unreality, or merely imaginary character.

If, on the contrary, a greater intensity, arising from a greater power of simple memory, should revive the feebler parts in repeated trains of thought, to the degree of attracting attention to them, and thus bringing them into a more distinct and vivid consciousness, there might arise an interest as to what they are, as to what are their relations, and where they belong, which would be able to inspire and guide an act of distinct reflection. A thought might thus be determined as a representative mental image; and such acts of reflection, inspired also by other motives more powerful than mere inquisitiveness, would by observation, analysis, and generalization (the counterparts of such outward processes in the merely animal mind) bring all such representative images, together with real memories and anticipations, into a single group, or subjective connection. The recognition of them in this connection is the knowledge of them as *my* thoughts, or *our* thoughts, or as phenomena of the mind.

When a thought, or an outward expression, acts in an animal's mind or in a man's, in the capacity of a sign, it carries forward the movements of a train, and directs attention away [p. 217] from itself to what it signifies or suggests; and consciousness is concentrated on the latter. But being sufficiently vivid in itself to engage distinct attention, it determines a new kind of action, and a new faculty of observation, of which the cerebral hemispheres appear to be the organs. From the action of these, in their more essential powers in memory and imagination, the objects or materials of reflection are also derived. Reflection would thus be, not what most metaphysicians appear to regard it, a fundamentally new faculty in man, as elementary and primordial as memory itself, or the power of abstractive attention, or the function of signs and representative images in generalization; but it would be determined in its contrasts with other mental faculties by the nature of its object·. On its subjective side it would he composed of the same mental faculties -- namely, memory, attention, abstraction -- as those which are employed in the primary use of the senses. It would be engaged upon what these senses have furnished to memory; but would act as independently of any orders of grouping and succession presented by them, as the several senses themselves do of one another. To this extent, reflection is a distinct faculty, and though, perhaps, not peculiar to man, is in him so prominent and marked in its effects on the development of the individual mind, that it may be regarded as his most essential and elementary mental distinction in kind. For differences of degrees in causes may make differences of kinds in effects.

Motives more powerful than mere inquisitiveness about the feebler steps or *mere* thoughts of a revived train, and more efficient in concentrating attention upon them, and upon their functions as signs, or suggesting images, would spring from the social nature of the animal, from the uses of mental communication between the members of a community, and from the *desire* to communicate, which these uses would create. And just as an outward sign associated with a mental image aids by its intensity in fixing attention upon the latter, so the *uses* of such outward signs and the motives connected with their employment would add *extensive* force, or interest, to the energy of attention in the cognition of this inward sign; [p. 218] and hence would aid in the reference of it and its sort to the subject *ego*, -- a being already known, or distinguished from other beings, as that which wills, desires, and feels. That which wills, desires, and feels is, in the more intelligent domestic animal, known by the proper name, which the animal recognizes and answers to by its actions, and is a consciousness of its individuality. It is not known or recognized by that most generic name "I"; since phenomena common to this individual and to others; or capable of being made common through the communications of language, are not distinctly referred to the individual self by that degree of abstractive attention and precision which an habitual exercise of the faculty of reflection is required to produce. But, in the same manner, the word "world," which includes the conscious subject in its meaning, would fail to suggest anything more to such an intelligence than more concrete terms do, -- such as what is around, within, near, or distant from consciousness; or it would fail to suggest the *whole* of that which philosophers divide into *ego* and *non-ego*, the outward and inward worlds. A contrast of this whole to its parts, however divided in predication, or the antithesis of subject and attributes, in a divisible unity and its component particulars, would not be suggested to an animal mind by the word "world." The "categories," or forms and conditions of human understanding, though doubtless innate in the naturalist's sense of the term, that is inherited, are only the ways and facilities of the higher exercise of the faculty of reflection. They are, doubtless, ways and facilities that are founded on the ultimate nature of mind; yet, on this very account, are universal, though only potential in the animal mind generally; just as the forms and conditions of *locomotion* are generally in the bodies of plants; forms and conditions founded on the ultimate natures or laws of motion, which would be exemplified in plants, if they also had the power of changing their positions, and are indeed exemplified in those forms of vegetable life that are transported, such as seeds, or can move and plant themselves, like certain spores.

The world of self-conscious intellectual activity, -- the world of mind, -- has, doubtless, its ultimate unconditional laws, everywhere [p. 219] exemplified in the actual phenomena of abstractive and reflective thought, and capable of being generalized in the reflective observations of the philosopher: and applied by him to the explanation of the phenomena of thought wherever manifested in outward expressions, whether in his fellow-men, or in the more intelligent dumb animals. Memory, in the effects of its more powerful and vivid revivals in the more intelligent animals, and especially in the case of large-brained man, presents this new world, in which the same faculties of observation, analysis, and generalization as those employed by intelligent beings in general, ascertain the marks and classes of phenomena strictly mental, and divide them, as a whole class, or *summum genus,* from those of the outward world. The distinction of subject and object becomes thus a classification through observation and analysis, instead of the intuitive distinction it is supposed to be by most metaphysicians. Intuitive to some extent, in one sense of the word, it doubtless is; that is, facilities and predispositions to associations, which are as effective as repeated experiences and observations would be, and which are inherited in the form of instincts, doubtless have much to do in bringing to pass this cognition, as well as many others, which appear to be innate, not only in the lower animals but also in man.

The very different aim of the evolutionist from that of his opponents -- the latter seeking to account for the *resemblances* of mental actions in beings supposed to be radically different in their mental constitutions, while the former seeks to account for the *differences* of manifestation in fundamentally similar mental constitutions-gives, in the theory of evolution, a philosophical *rôle* to the word "instinct," and to its contrast with intelligence, much inferior to that which this contrast has had in the discussions of the mental faculties of animals. For the distinction of instinct and intelligence, though not less real and important in the classification of actions in psycho-zoölogy, and as important even as that of animal and vegetable is in general zoölogy, or the distinctions of organic and inorganic, living and dead, in the general science of life, is yet, like these, in its applications a vague and ill-defined distinction, and is most profitably [p. 220] studied in the subordinate classes of actions, and in the special contrasts which are summarized by it. Under the naturalist's point of view, the contrasts of dead and living matters, inorganic and organic products, vegetable and animal forms and functions, automatic and sentient movements, instinctive and intelligent motives and actions, are severally rough divisions of *series*, which are clearly enough contrasted in their extremities, but ill defined at their points of division. Thus, we have the long series beginning with the processes of growth, nutrition, and waste, and in movements independent of nervous connections, and continued in processes in which sensations are involved, first vaguely, as in the processes of digestion, circulation, and the general stimulative action of the nervous system; then distinctly, as in the stimulative sensations of respiration, winking, swallowing, coughing, and sneezing, more or less under general control or the action of the will. This series is continued, again, into those sensations, impulses, and consequent actions which are wholly controllable, though spontaneously arising; and thence into the motives to action which are wholly dependent on, or involved in, the immediate controlling powers of the will, -- a series in which the several marks of distinction are clearly enough designated in the abstract, as the colors of the spectrum are by their names, but are not clearly separated in the concrete applications of them.

Again, we have the series of voluntary actions, beginning at the connections between perceptions, emotions, and consequent actions, which are strictly instinctive. These, though inherited, are independent of the effects of higher, and more properly voluntary, actions in the individual's progenitors, as well as in himself When they are not simple ultimate and universal laws of mental natures, or elementary mental connections, they are combinations produced through their serviceableness to life, or by natural selection and exercise, that is in the same general manner in which bodily organs, powers, and functions are produced or altered. Such connections between perceptions, emotions, and consequent actions, derived through natural selection, or even those that are ultimate laws, and determine, in a manner not peculiar to any species, the conditions [p. 221] and uses of serviceable actions,--are *instinctive* connections, or powers of *instinct,* in a restricted but perfectly definite use of the word. But following immediately in the series of voluntary actions are, first, the inherited effects of habits, and next, habits properly so called, or effects produced by higher voluntary actions in the individual. *Habits* properly so called, and *dispositions,* which are the inherited effects of habits, are not different in their practical character or modes of action from true instincts; but differ only in their origin and capacity of alteration through the higher forms of volition. The latter, or proper, volitions are connections between the occasions, or external means and conditions of an action, and the production of the action itself through the *motive of the end*, and not through emotions or by any other ties instinctively uniting them. They are joined by the foreseen ulterior effect of the action, or else through a union produced by its influence. The desirableness of what is effected by an action connects its occasions, or present means and conditions, with the action itself, and causes its production through the end felt in imagination. The influence of the end, or ulterior motive in volition, may not be a consciously recognized part of the action, or a distinctly separated step in it, and will actually cease to be the real tie when a series of repeated volitions has established a habit, or a fixed association between them and their occasions, or external conditions. This connection in habits is, as we have said, closely similar to strictly instinctive connections, and is indistinguishable from them independently of questions of origin and means of alterations.

Independently of these questions, the series of voluntary actions starting from the strictly instinctive joins to them natural dispositions, or the inherited effects of habit, and passes on to habits properly so called, thence into those in which the ulterior motives of true volitions are still operative, though not as separate parts of consciousness, and thence on to mere faculties of action, or to those actions in which such a motive is still the sole effective link, though quite faded out of distinct attention, or attended to with a feeble and intermittent consciousness. Thence it comes finally to the distinct recognition in reflective [p. 222] thought of an ulterior motive to an action. The ulterior motive, the end or good to be effected by an action, anticipated in imagination, joins the action to its present means and conditions in actual volitions, or else joins it in imagination with some future occurrence of them in an *intention,* or a predetermination of the will. These ulterior motives, ends, or determinations of an action through foreseen consequences of it, may be *within* the will, in the common and proper meaning of the word, when it is spoken of as free, or unconstrained by an outward force, or necessity; or they may be *without* it, like instinctive tendencies to which the will is said to *consent* or *yield,* as well as in other cases to be *opposed.* The motives within the will, either distinctly or vaguely operative, or completely superseded by *forces* of habit, constitute the individual's character.

To summarize all the steps and contrasts of these series under the general heads of intelligence and instinct would be, from the evolutionist's and naturalist's point of view, only a rough classification, like that of living beings into animals and plants; and any attempts at investigating the distinctions and classes of mental natures by framing elaborate definitions of this summary contrast would be like concentrating all the energies of scientific pursuit in biography, and staking its success on the question whether the sponge be an animal or a plant. This is, in fact, the scholastic method, from which modern science is comparatively, and fortunately, set free; being contented with finding out more and more about beings that are unmistakably animals or plants, and willing to study the nature of the sponge by itself, and defer the classification of it to the end. The more ambitious scholastic method is followed in the science of psycho-zoölogy by those who seek, in an ultimate definition of this sort, to establish an impassable barrier between the minds of men and those of the lower animals, -- being actuated apparently by the naive, though generous, motive of rendering the former more respectable, or else of defending a worth in them supposed to be dependent on such a barrier. This aim would be confusing at least, if not a false one, in a strictly scientific inquiry. [p. 223]

Although the definition of the subject world through the distinction in memory of the phenomena of signification from those of outward perception, would be a classification spontaneously arising through inherited facilities and predispositions to associations, which are as effective as repeated experiences would be, it must still be largely aided by the voluntary character of outward signs, -- vocal, gestural, and graphic, -- by which all signs are brought under the control of the will, or of that most central, active personality, which is thus connected externally and actively, as well as through the memory, with the inward signs or the representative mental images. These images are brought by this association under stronger and steadier attention; their character, as representative images or signs, is more distinctly seen in reflection, and they are not any longer merely guides in thought, blindly followed. They form, by this association, a little representative world arising to thought at will. Command of language is an important condition of the effective cognition of a sign as such. It is highly probable that the dog not only cannot utter the sound "fox," but cannot revive the sound as heard by him. The word cannot, therefore, be of aid to him in fixing his attention in reflection on the mental image of the fox as seen or smelt by him. But the latter, spontaneously arising, would be sufficient to produce a lively train of thoughts, or a vivid dream. · It by no means follows from his deficiencies of vocal and auditory imagination that the dog has not, in some directions, aid from outward signs, and some small degree of reflective power, though this, probably, falls far short of the clear division of the two worlds realized in the cognition of "*cogito.*" Thus, he has at command the outward sign of the chase, incipient movements of his limbs, such as he makes in his dreams; and this may make the mental image of the chase, with its common obstacles and incidents, distinct in his imagination, in spite of the greater interest which carries the thoughts of his dream forward to the end of the pursuit, the capture of the game. He may even make use of this sign, as he in fact does when he indicates to his master by his movements his eagerness for a walk or for the chase. [p. 224]

Command of signs, and, indeed, all the volitional or active powers of an animal, including attention in perception, place it in relation to outward things in marked contrast with its passive relations of sensation and inattentive or passive perception. The distinctness, or prominence, in consciousness given by an animal's attention to its perceptions, and the greater energy given by its intentions or purposes to its outward movements, cannot fail to afford a ground of discrimination between these as causes, both of inward and outward events, and those outward causes which are not directly under such control, but form an independent system, or several distinct systems, of causes. This would give rise to a form of self-consciousness more immediate and simple than the intellectual one, and is apparently realized in dumb animals. They, probably, do not have, or have only in an indistinct and ineffective form, the intellectual cognitions of *cogito* and *sum*; but having reached the cognition of a contrast in subject and object as *causes* both in inward and outward events, they have already acquired a form of subjective consciousness, or a knowledge of the *ego.* That they do not, and cannot, name it, at least by a general name, or understand it by the general name of "I" or *ego,* comes from the absence of the attributes of *ego* which constitute the intellectual self-consciousness, A dog can, nevertheless, understand the application of his own proper name to himself, both in the direct and the indirect reference of our language to his conduct or his wants; and can also understand the application to himself of the general name, -- "dog." He cannot say, "I am a dog," and probably has but the faintest, if any, understanding of what the proposition would mean if he could utter it; though he probably has as much understanding, at least, as the parrot has in saying, "I am Poll." For there are, in these propositions, two words expressing the abstractest ideas that the human mind can reach. One of them, "I," is the name of one of the two *summa genera, ego* and *non-ego,* into which human consciousness is divisible. "I am a dog," and "Camp is a dog," would mean much the same to Camp; just as "I am a child," and "John is a child" are not clearly distinguished by John even after he has acquired considerable [p. 225] command of language. The other word, "am," is a form of the substantive verb expressing existence in general, but further determined to express the *present* existence of the *speaker* or *subject.* These further determinations, in tense, number, and persons, are, however, the most important parts of meaning in the various forms of the substantive verb to the common and barbarous minds, from which we and the philosophical grammarian have received them. The substantive verb is, accordingly, irregular in most languages under the form of a grammatical paradigm. In this form the philosophical grammarian subordinates to the infinitive meaning of a word those determinations which, in the invention of words, were apparently regarded as leading ideas in many other cases as well as in the substantive verb, and were expressed by words with distinct etymologies.

Not only the dog and other intelligent dumb animals, but some of the least advanced among human beings? also, are unable to arrive at a distinct abstraction of what is expressed by "to be," or "to exist." Being is concreted, or determined, to such minds down, at least, to the conception of living or acting; to a conception scarcely above what is implied in the actions of the more intelligent animals, namely, their apprehension of themselves as agents or patients with wills and feelings distinct from those of other animals, and from the forces and interests of outward nature generally. "Your dog is here, or is coming, and at your service," is a familiar expression in the actions of dogs not remarkable for intelligence. A higher degree of· abstraction and generalization than the simple steps, which are sufficient, as we have seen, for inference in enthymematic reasonings to particular conclusions, would be required in reflection; and a more extensive and persistent exercise of the faculty of reflection, aided by voluntary signs or by language, than any dumb animal attains to, would be needed to arrive at the cognition of cogito and *sum.* This is a late acquisition with children; and it would, indeed, be surprising if the mind of a dumb animal should attain to it. But there is little ground in this for believing, with most metaphysicians, that the cognition is absolutely *sui generis,* or an ultimate and underived [p. 226] form of knowledge; or that it is not approached gradually, as well as realized with different degrees of clearness and precision, as the faculty of reflection becomes more and more exercised.

That a dumb animal should not know itself to be a thinking being, is hardly more surprising than that it should not be aware of the circulation of its blood and other physiological functions; or that it should not know the anatomy of its frame or that of its nervous system, or the seat of its mental faculties, or the fact that the brain is much smaller in it, in proportion to the size of its body, than in man. Its reflective observation may be as limited in respect to the phenomena of thought as the outward observation of most men is in respect to these results of scientific research. And, on the other hand, the boasted intellectual self-consciousness of man is a knowledge of a subject, not through all its attributes and phenomena, but only through enough of them in general to determine and distinguish it from outward objects, and make it serve as the subject of further attributions or predications, as reflective observation makes them known. The abstract forms of this knowledge, the laws of logic and grammar, and the categories of the understanding, which are forms of all scientific knowledge, are all referable to the action of a *purpose* to know, and to fix knowledge by precise generalization; just as the mechanical conditions of flight are referable to the purpose to fly and to secure the requisite means. Generalization already exists, however, with particular acts of inquisitiveness in the animal mind; and there is required only the proper degree of attention to signs in order to make it act in accordance with laws which, *if they are universal and necessary laws of the mind,* are equally laws of the animal intelligence, though not actually exemplified in it; just as the laws of locomotion are not actually exemplified in the bodies of plants, but are still potential in them.

The inferior and savage races of men, whose languages do not include any abstract terms like truth, goodness, and sweetness, but only concrete ones, like true, good, and sweet, would hardly be able to form a conception, even a vague and obscure [p. 227] one, of the mystic's research of omniscience in the profundities of self-consciousness. They ought on this account, perhaps, to be regarded as races distinct from that of these philosophers, at least mentally, and to be classed, in spite of their powers of speech and limited vocabularies, with the dumb, but still intelligent, animals. If, however, the theory above propounded be true, this greatest of human qualities, intelligent self-consciousness, understood in its actual and proper limits, would follow as a consequence of a greater brain, a greater, or more powerful and vivid, memory and imagination, bringing to light, as it were, and into distinct consciousness, phenomena of thought which reflective observation refers to the subject, already known in the dumb animal, or distinguished as an active cause from the forces of outward nature, and from the wills of other animals. The degrees of abstraction and the successively higher and higher steps of generalization, the process which, in scientific knowledge, brings not only the particulars of experience under general designations, but, with a conscious purpose, brings the less general under the more general, or gives common names not only to each and all resembling objects and relations, but also more general common names to what is denoted by these names, thus grouping them under higher categories, --this process brings together the several forms of self-consciousness. Willing, desiring, feeling, and lastly thinking, also, are seen in thought to belong together, or to the same subject; and by thinking they are brought under a common view and receive a common name, or several common names, to wit, "my mind," "me," "I," "my mental states."

By still further observation, comparison, and analysis on the part of philosophers, this step is seen to be the highest degree of abstraction, since nothing appears to be common to all my mental states, except their belonging together and acting on one another, along with their common independence of other existences in this mutual action. The word "I" is discovered by philosophers to be a word without meaning or determination, or to be as meaningless as the words "thing," "being," "existence," which are subjects stripped of all attributes. "I" [p. 228] is the bare subject of mental phenomena. The word points them out, but does not declare anything of their nature by its meaning, essence, or implied attribution, which is, in fact, no meaning at all. Hence philosophers have placed this term, or name, over against that which is not, or in contrast with all other existences. Common language has no name for the latter, and so philosophers were compelled to call it the *non-ego,* in order to contrast these two highest categories, or *summa genera,* into which they divide all of which we are, or may be, conscious. Grammatical science, however, furnished convenient substitutes for these words. *Ego* and *non-ego* were named "subject" and "object." Yet these terms so applied do not retain any meanings. "Subject" is applicable to denote the *ego,* rather than the *non-ego,* only because it is the positive or more prominent term of the antithesis in its grammatical application, like "active and passive." Sir William Hamilton undertakes, however, to assign them meanings in psychology by representing the *object* as that which *is thought about,* and the *subject* as that which *thinks,* or *acts,* or that in which the thought or action inheres. But this definition is given from the active subject's point of view, and not from the whole scope of the subject-attributes. We act, indeed, in volition and attentive perception on the outer world or *non-ego;·* but in sensation and passive perception we are the objects influenced, governed, or acted on by this outer world. Moreover. from the point of view of the effects of thinking, both the *object* and *subject* are the subjects of attribution. We attribute qualities to external objects, and, at the same time, to their mental images, which, in their capacity as representative images, or internal signs of objects and relations, are called up and separately attended to in the human consciousness, and are, in turn, referred or attributed to the conscious subject, or to its memory and understanding.

These images, in their *individual* capacity, are not to be distinguished, even in human consciousness, from the object of perception.. It is in their specific, or notative, function as signs, and as referring back to memories of like experiences, which they summarize, that they are separately and subjectively cognized. [p. 229] *Individually* they are divisible only into real and unreal, or into remembered and imagined combinations of particular impressions. As inward and mine they are "concepts," or thoughts directing the processes of thought, and are specially related to my will and its motives. The classification of events as inward and outward does not necessarily imply that the scientific process depends on each man's experiences of their connections alone; for the forms of language, and what is indirectly taught in learning a language, guide observation in this matter largely; and so, also, very probably, do inherited aptitudes, ties, or tendencies to combination, which have the same effect in associating the particulars of the individual's experiences as the frequent repetitions of them in himself would have, and are, indeed, by the theory of evolution, the consequences of such repeated experiences in the individual's progenitors. Such a reference of the distinction of subject and object to instinctive tendencies in our minds is not equivalent to the metaphysical doctrine that this distinction is intuitive. For this implies more than is meant by the word "instinctive" from the naturalist's point of view. It implies that the cognition is absolute; independent not only of the individual's experiences, but of all possible previous experience, and has a certainty, reality, and cogency that no amount of experience could give to an empirical classification.

The metaphysical dogmas, for which this formula is given, deserve but a passing scientific consideration. Truths independent of all experience are not known to exist, unless we exclude from what we mean by "experience" that experience which we have in learning the meanings of words and in agreeing to definitions and the conventions of language, on the ground that they depend solely, or may be considered as depending solely, on a lexical authority, from which a kind of necessity proceeds, independent of reality in the relations and connections of the facts denoted by the words. It is possible that laws exist absolutely universal, binding fate and infinite power as well as speech and the intelligible use of words; but it is not possible that the analytical processes of any finite intellect should discover what particular laws these are. Such [p. 230] an intellect may legislate with absolute freedom in the realm of definition and word-making, provided it limits itself to its autonomy, and does not demand of other intellects that they shall be governed by such laws as if they were of universal application in the world of common experience. It is also possible that beliefs, or convictions, exist, supposed by the mystic to be independent of all ordinary forms of particular experience, "which no amount of experience could produce"; but it is not true that there are any universal or scientific beliefs of this kind. The effects of inherited aptitudes, and of early, long-continued, and constantly repeated experiences in the individual, together with the implications of language itself, in fixing and in giving force and certainty to an idea or a belief, have, probably, not been sufficiently considered by those metaphysicians who claim a preternatural and absolute origin for certain of our cognitions; and also, perhaps, the more dogmatic among these thinkers over-estimate the force and certainty of the beliefs, or mistake the *kind* of necessity they have. The essential importance, the necessity and universality in language, of pronominal words or signs, should not be mistaken for a real *a priori* necessity in the relations expressed by them. Meta-physicians should consider that *ego* and *non-ego*, as real existences, are not individual phenomena, but groups with demonstrative names the least possible determined in meaning, or are the most abstract subjects of the phenomena of experience, though determined, doubtless, in their applications partly by spontaneous, instinctive, or natural and inherited tendencies to their formation.

This view of the origin of the cognition of *cogito* is equally opposed to the schemes of "idealism" and "natural realism," which divide modem schools of philosophy. According to the "idealists," the conscious subject is immediately known, at least in its phenomena, and the phenomena are intuitively known to belong to it; while the existence of anything external to the mind is an inference from the phenomena of self, or a reference of some of them to external causes. Objects are only known mediately "by their effects on *us*." Against this view the "natural realist" appeals effectively to the common-sense, or [p. 231] natural judgment of unsophisticated minds, and is warranted by this judgment in declaring that the object of consciousness is *just as immediately* known as the subject is.   But natural realism goes beyond this judgment and holds that both the subject and object are absolutely, immediately, and equally known through their essential attributes in perception. This is more than an unlearned jury are competent to say. For if by immediacy we mean the relation which a particular *unattributed* phenomenon has to consciousness in general, we are warranted in saying that immediately, or without the step of attribution, subject and object are undistinguished in consciousness. Thus, the sensations of sound and color and taste and pleasure and pain, and the emotions of hope and fear and love and hate, *if not yet referred to their causes, or even classified as sensations and emotions*, belong to neither world exclusively. But so far as any man can remember, no such unattributed or unclassified states of consciousness are experienced. He cannot say, however, that they cannot exist, or (what is worse for the theory) that a state of consciousness cannot be wrongly attributed or classified. All states of consciousness are, it is true, referred to one or the other, or partly to each of the two worlds; and this attribution is, in part at least, instinctive, yet not independent of all experience, since it comes either from the direct observation of our progenitors, or, possibly, through the natural selection of them; that is, possibly through the survival of those who rightly divided the worlds, and did not often mistake a real danger for a dream or for an imagined peril, nor often mistake a dream of security for real safety. If, however, we mean by immediacy such an instinctive attribution, independent of repeated connections of attributes in their subject through the individual's own experiences, then "natural realism" is most in accordance with our view, with such exceptions as the mistakes and corrections of dreams and hallucinations imply, and excepting the ontological or metaphysical positions that are assumed in it.

If the natural realist is not also an evolutionist (and usually he is not), then his meaning of intuitions must be that they are absolute and underived universal facts of connection in [p. 232] phenomena. He must suppose that distinct phenomena have stamped upon them indelible marks of their ultimate highest class, equivalents for "I" and "not-I," as the individuals of a herd of cattle are branded with the mark of their owner. Such an immutable mark would, however, render the mistakes of insanity, hallucinations, and dreams impossible, or else would refer them (as has actually been supposed[4]) to the mystery of the existence of evil, -- a convenient disposition of philosophical puzzles. In the doctrine of evolution the meaning of the word "intuition " does not imply immutability in the connections of instinctively combined phenomena, except where such connection is an ultimate law of nature, or is the simplest causal connection, like the laws of motion, or the laws of logic, regarding logic as a science and not merely as an art. The intuition of space in the blind might be, from this point of view, a different combination of sensibilities from that in other men; and the interpretation of sensations of hearing or sight in hallucinations as being caused by outward objects, when, in reality, they. arise from disturbances or abnormal conditions of the nervous system, would not be an interpretation involving violations of ultimate laws, or suspensions in rebellious Nature of relations between cause and effect. Variations in intuitions and instinctive judgments would be as natural and explicable as errors of judgment are in the experiences of the individual man. But the doctrine of natural realism, independently of that of evolution and the implied mutability of instincts, has insurmountable difficulties.

Idealism, on the other hand, appears to contradict not the abnormal, so much as the common, phenomena of consciousness. It seems to be related to the modern sciences of physics and physiology very nearly as natural realism is to scholastic logic and ontology. Dating from the time of Descartes, it appears, in all its forms, to depend on a more exact knowledge of the bodily apparatus and outward physical causes of perception than the ancients possessed. This knowledge made it evident that perception, and even sensation, are fully determined or realized in the brain only through other parts of the [p. 233] bodily apparatus, and through outward forces and movements like those of pressure and vibration. That the perception, or sensation, is experienced, or is seated, in the brain, was a natural and proper conclusion. That the apparent object of perception is not only distant from what thus appeared to be the seat of the perception, but that a long series of usually unknown, or unnoticed, movements intervenes between it and this apparent seat,-these facts gave great plausibility   to a confused interpretation of the phenomena, namely, that the perception is first realized as a state of the conscious *ego*, and, afterwards, is referred to the outward world through the associations of general experience, as an effect produced upon us by an otherwise unknown outward cause. On similar grounds a similar misinterpretation was made of the phenomena of volition, namely, that a movement in ourselves, originally and intuitively known to be *ours*, produces an effect in the outward world at a distance from us, through the intervention of a series of usually unknown (or only indirectly known) agencies. Remote effects of the outer world on us, and our actions in producing remote effects on it, appeared to be the first or intuitive elements in our knowledge of these phenomena, all the rest being derived or inferential. This was to confound the seat of sensation or perception in the brain with its proper subjectivity, or the reference of it to the subject.

The position in the brain where the last physical condition for the production of a sensation is situated is, no doubt, properly called the place or seat of the sensation, especially as it is through the movements of the brain with other special nervous tracts, and independently of any movements out of the nervous system, that like sensations are, or can be, revived, though these revived ones are generally feebler than those that are set in movement by outward forces. Nevertheless, this physiological seat of a sensation is no part of our direct knowledge of it. *A priori* we cannot assign it any place nor decide that it has, or has not, a place. The place which we do assign it, in case it is outward, is the place determined by a great variety of sensations and active forms of consciousness experienced in the [p. 234] localization of the object to which it is referred. It is only by the association (either spontaneous and instinctive, or acquired) of this sensation with those sensations and actions that are involved in the localization of the object, that we arrive at any notion of its locality. If we do not form any such associations of it with otherwise determined localities, and if it and its kind remain after much experience unlocalized, or only vaguely localized in our bodies, it is then, *but not till then,* referred to the conscious self as a subjective phenomenon. There remains the alternative, of course, in the theory of evolution, that the negative experiences, which would thus determine the subjective character of a phenomenon, may be the experiences of our progenitors, and that our judgment of this character may be, in many cases, an instinctive one, arising from the inherited effects of these former experiences. Otherwise this judgment in the individual mind, and from its own experiences, would appear to be posterior, in point of time, to its acquaintance with the object world, since this judgment would be determined by the *absence* of any uniform connection in the phenomenon with the phenomena of locality. Instead of, being, as the theories of idealism hold, first known as' a phenomenon of the subject *ego*, or as an effect upon us of an hypothetical outward world, its first unattributed condition would be, by our view, one of neutrality between the two worlds.

In dissenting, therefore, from both extremes, -- the theory of idealism and that of natural realism, or assenting to the latter only as qualified by the theory of evolution, -- I have supposed both theories to be dealing with the two worlds only as worlds of phenomena, without considering the metaphysical bearings and varieties of them with respect to the question of the cognition of non-phenomenal existences, on the grounds of belief in an inconceivable and metaphysical matter or spirit; for, according to the view proposed as a substitute for these extremes, subject and object are only names of the highest classes, and are not the names of inconceivable substrata of phenomena. Ontology or metaphysics would not be likely to throw much original light on the scientific evolution of self-consciousness; but it becomes itself an interesting object of [p. 235] study as a phase of this evolution seen in the light of science. When one comes to examine in detail the supposed cognitions of super-sensible existences, and the faculty of necessary truth which is called" the reason," or else is described in its supposed results as the source of necessary beliefs or convictions, or of natural and valid hypotheses of inconceivable realities, great difficulty is experienced, on account of the abstract character of the beliefs, in distinguishing what is likely to be strictly inherited from what is early and uniformly acquired in the development of the faculty· of reflection, and especially from what is imbibed through language, the principal philosophical instrument of this faculty. The languages employed by philosophers are themselves lessons in ontology, and have, in their grammatical structures, implied conceptions and beliefs common to the philosopher and to the barbarian inventors of language, as well as other implications which the former takes pains to avoid. How much besides he ought to avoid, in the correction of conceptions erroneously derived from the forms of language, is a question always important to be considered in metaphysical inquiries.

The conception of *substance,* as a nature not fully involved in the contrast of essential and accidental attributes, and the connection, or co-existence, of them in our experiences; or the conception of substance as also implying the real, though latent, co-existence of all attributes in an existence unknown to us, or known only in a non-phenomenal and inconceivable way, -- this conception needs to be tested by an examination of the possible causes of it as an effect of the forms of language and other familiar associations, which, however natural, may still be misleading. To the minds of the barbarian inventors of language, words had not precise meanings, for definition is not a barbarian accomplishment. Hence, to such minds, definite and precise attributions, as of sweetness to honey and sugar, or light to the day, to the heavenly bodies, or to fire, are strongly in contrast with the vagueness which appears to them inherent in substantive names, -- inherent not as vagueness, however, but as *something else.* Such names did not clearly distinguish persons and things, for the day and the heavenly bodies were [p. 236] personal, and fire apparently was an animal or a spirit. Removing as much as possible of mere crudeness from such conceptions, predication would yet appear to be a reference of something distinctly known to something essentially unknown, or known only by one or a few attributes needed to distinguish it by a name, as proper names distinguish persons. The meaning of this name, and the conception of it as meaning much more, and as actually referring to unapparent powers of bringing to light attributes previously unknown, -- powers manifested in an actual effect when a new attribute is added in predication, -- this vague, ill-defined, and essentially hidden meaning is assimilated in grammar, and thence in philosophy, to an agent putting forth a new manifestation of itself in a real self-assertion.

The contrast of "active and passive" in the forms of verbs illustrates how the barbaric mind mounted into the higher regions of abstraction in language through concrete imaginations. The subject of a proposition, instead of being thought of as that vaguely determined group of phenomena with which the predicate is found to be connected, was thought either to perform an *action* on an object as expressed through the transitive verb, or to be acted on by the object as expressed through the passive form, or to put forth an action absolute, expressed by the neuter verb, or to assert its past, present, or future existence absolutely, and its possession of certain properties as expressed by the substantive verb, and by the copula and predicate. This personification of the subject of a proposition, which is still manifested in the forms and terminology of grammar, is an assimilation of things to an active, or at least demonstrative, self-consciousness or personality. It had hardly reached the degree of abstraction needed for the clear intellectual self-consciousness of *cogito.* It rather implied that things also think. The invention of substantive names for attributes, that is, abstract names, like goodness or truth, -- an invention fraught with most important consequences to human knowledge,--brought at first more prominently forward the realistic tendencies which philosophers have inherited from the barbarian inventors of language. Abstract names do not seem to have been meant at [p. 237] first to be the direct names of attributes, or collections of attributes, as " goodness " and "humanity," but to be the names of powers (such as make things good, or make men what they are), names which appear to be results of the earliest conscious or scientific analysis in the progress of the human mind, but which are strongly tainted still by the barbaric conception of words as the names of active beings. Abstract words were not, however, as active or demonstrative as their savage progenitors, the concrete general substantives. They appear rather as artificers, or the agents which build up things, or make them what they are. But, by means of them, concrete general names were deprived of their powers and reduced to subjection. To have direct general names, and to have general powers, seem to be synonymous to savage and semi-barbarous mind.

I have spoken as if all this were a matter of past history, instead of being an actually present state of philosophical thought, and a present condition of some words in the minds of many modern thinkers. The misleading metaphors are, it is true, now recognized as metaphors; but their misleading character is not clearly seen to its full extent. The subjects of propositions are still made to do the work, to bear the impositions, to make known tile properties and accidents expressed by their predicates, or to assert their own existence and autonomy, just so far as they are supposed to be the names of anything but the assemblages of known essential qualities or phenomena actually co-existent in our experiences, that is of the qualities which their definitions involve, and to which other attributes are added (but from which they are not evolved) in real predication; or just so far as they are supposed to be the names of unknown and imperceptible entities. Names are directly the designations of things, not of hidden powers, or wills, in things. But it is not necessary to regard them as precisely definable, or as connoting definite groups of qualities or the essential attributes of things, in order that they may fulfill the true functions of words; for they are still only the names of things, not of wills in things, on the one hand, nor of "concepts" or thoughts in us, on the other hand. They are synonyms of "concepts," if we please to extend synonymy so as [p. 238] to include the whole range of the *signs* of things; but both the "concept" and its verbal synonym may be, and generally are, *vague*. For just as in the major premises of syllogisms the subject is, in general, a co-designation of two undivided parts of a class of objects, one known directly to have, or lack, the attributes affirmed or denied in this premise, and the other part, judged by induction to be also possessed, or not possessed of them, -- a co-designation in which the conclusion of the syllogism is virtually contained, so as to make the syllogism appear to be a *petitio principii* (as it would be but for this implied induction[5]), -- so in the simple naming of objects the names may be properly regarded as the names of groups of qualities, in which groups the qualities are partly known and partly unknown, predication in real (not verbal) propositions being the conversion of the latter into the former. But in this view of the functions of words, it is necessary, at least, to suppose enough of the known attributes of objects to be involved in the meanings of their names to make the applications of the names distinct and definite. Names, with the capacity they would thus acquire, or have actually had, in spite of metaphysics, of having their meanings modified or changed, are best adapted to the functions of words in promoting the progress of knowledge. From this use of words their essences, both the apparent and the inscrutable, have disappeared altogether, except so far as the actual existence and co-existence of the known attributes of objects are implied by names, or so far as the co-existence of these with previously unknown ones is also implied by the use of names as the subjects of propositions. No inscrutable powers in words or things, nor any immutable connections among the attributes called essential, are thus imposed upon the use of words in science.

Metaphysicians, on the other hand, in nearly all that is left to the peculiar domain of their inquiries, possess their problems and solutions in certain words, such as "substance," "cause," "matter," "mind," which still retain, at least in metaphysical usage, the barbaric characters we have examined. Matter and mind, for example, still remain, not only with metaphysicians, [p. 239] but also with the vulgar, designations of unknown inscrutable powers in the outward and inward worlds, or powers which, according to semi, are known only to a higher form of intuition through the faculty of "Reason"; or, being really inscrutable and inconceivable by any human faculty, as others hold, are, nevertheless, regarded as certainly existent, and attested by irresistible natural beliefs. That beliefs in beings, unknown and unknowable, are real beliefs, and are natural (though more so to some minds than to others), seems *a priori* probable on the theory of evolution, without resorting to the effects of early training and the influence of associations in language itself, by which the existence of such beliefs is accounted for by some scientific philosophers. But the authority which the theory of evolution would assign to these beliefs is that of the conceptions which barbarous and vulgar minds have formed of the functions of words, and of the natures which they designate. Inheritance of these conceptions, that is, of aptitudes or tendencies to their formation, and the continued action of the causes so admirably analyzed by Mr. Mill,[6] through which he proposes to account for these beliefs directly, and which have retained, especially in the metaphysical conception of "matter," the barbarian's feelings and notions about real existence as a power to produce phenomena, are sufficient to account for the existence of these beliefs and their cogency, without assigning them any force as authorities.

That some minds have inherited these beliefs, or the tendency to form them, more completely than others, accords with a distinction in the mental characters of philosophers which Professor Masson makes in his work on Recent British Philosophy, and illustrates by the philosophies of Mr. Carlyle, Sir W. Hamilton, and Mr. Mill, namely, the differences arising from the degrees in which the several thinkers were actuated by an "ontological faith," or an "ontological feeling or passion," which, according to Professor Masson, has in the history of the world amounted to "a rage of ontology," and has been the motive of wars and martyrdoms. This passion would appear, [p. 240] according to the theory of evolution, to be a survival of the barbarian's feelings and notions of phenomena as the outward show of hidden powers in things, analogous to his own expressions in language and gesture of his will or interior activity. As he assigned his own name, or else the name "I," to this active inward personality, and not to the group of external characters by which he was known to his fellow-barbarians; and as he also named and addressed them as indwelling spirits, so he seemed to apply his general designations of things. The traces of this way of regarding names and things, surviving in the grammatical inventions and forms of speech, which the barbarian has transmitted to us, include even the sexes of things. The metaphysical meanings of the terms "substance," "matter," "mind," "spirit," and "cause" are other traces. The metaphysical realism of abstract terms appears, in like manner, to be a trace of an original analysis of motives in the powers of things to produce their phenomena, analogous to the barbarian's analysis of motives in his own will or those of his fellows.

According to Professor Masson, Sir W. Hamilton was strongly actuated by "the ontological passion." This would mean, according to our interpretation of it, that he had inherited, or had partly, perhaps, imbibed from his philosophical studies, the barbarian's mode of thought. And it appeared in the metaphysical extension which he gave to the doctrine of natural realism, which, with him, was not merely the doctrine of the equal immediacy and the instinctive attribution of subjective and objective phenomena, but included also natural beliefs in the equal and independent, though hidden, existences of the metaphysical substrata of matter and mind. He was, nevertheless, so far influenced by modern scientific modes of thought that he did not claim for these natural beliefs at all the character of cognitions, nor did he claim determinate conception of these existences except as to their mutual independence. He rejected the metaphysician's invention of a faculty of "reason," cognizant of supersensible realities; and really contradicted himself in claiming, with most modem thinkers, that knowledge of phenomena, is the only possible knowledge, [p. 241] while he held that belief in what could not thus be known had the certainty of knowledge, and was in effect knowledge, though he did not call it knowledge.[7]

Another point in Sir W. Hamilton's philosophy illustrates our theory on a different side. While contending for the equal immediacy of our knowledge of subject and object, he, nevertheless, held that the phenomena of the subject had a superior certainty to those of the object, on the ground that the latter could be doubted (as they were by certain idealists) without logical contradiction, while the former could not be, since to doubt the existence of the subject would be to doubt the doubt, and thus neutralize it. To say nothing of other objections to this as a criterion of subjective certainty, it is obvious that it has no cogency as applied to the metaphysical, or non-phenomenal, existence of the subject. To doubt that a doubt inheres in a non-phenomenal subject, is not to doubt the existence of the doubt itself as a phenomenon, or even as a phenomenon referable to the subject group of phenomena. In regard to the impossibility of doubting the existence of this subject group, which, as including the doubt itself, would thus neutralize it, we ought to distinguish between a doubt of a doubt as a mere phenomenon of consciousness generally, that is as unattributed either to subject or object, and the doubt of the validity of the attribution of it to the subject. There can be logical contradiction only in respect to attribution, either explicit or implicit, and so far as the doubt is merely a phenomenon of which nothing is judged or known but its actual existence in consciousness, a doubt of it, though impossible, is yet not so on grounds of' logical contradiction. Its actual presence would be the only proof of its presence, its actual absence the only proof of its absence. But this is equally true of all phenomena in consciousness, generally. If in reflection we examine whether a color of any sort is present, we have inquired, not merely about the bare existence of a phenomenon of which the phenomenon itself could alone assure us, but about its classes, whether it is a color or not, and what sort of a color; and we should attribute it, if present, to the object world, or the object group of [p. 242] phenomena, by the very same sort, if not with the same degree, of necessity which determines the attribution of a doubt to the subject-consciousness. If now, having attributed the color or the doubt to its proper world, we should call in question the existence of this world, we should contradict ourselves; and this would be the case equally whether the attribution was made to the outward world, as of the color, or to the inward world, as of the doubt.

There may be different kinds of reflective doubt about either phenomenon. We should not ordinarily be able to question seriously whether the doubt belonged to the class "doubts," its resemblance to others of the class beings a relation of phenomena universal and too clear to be dismissed from attention; and the color would call up its class with equal cogency, as well as the class of surfaces or spaces in which it appears always inherent. But we might doubt, nevertheless, seriously and rationally, whether a doubt had arisen from rational considerations in our minds, or from a disease of the nervous system, from hypochondriasis, or low spirits. So also in regard to the color and the forms in which it appears embodied, we may reasonably question whether the appearance[*sic*] has arisen from causes really external, or from disease, as in hallucinations.

There remains one other source of misunderstanding about the comparative certainty of "I think," and of that which I think about. The attributions contained in the latter may be particular, empirical, and unfamiliar, or based on a very limited experience and on *this account* may be uncertain; while the very general and highest attribution of the thought to myself will be most certain. The superior certainty of the clause "I think" over that which I think about disappears, however, as soon as the latter is made an attribution of equal simplicity, generality, and breadth in my experience; as when I say, "I think that there is an outer world," or, "I think that beings beside me exist." "To think that I think," is not more properly the formula of consciousness in general than "To think that a being not-I is thought about." It is not even the complete formula of *self-consciousness*, which, as we have seen, has several forms not necessarily coeval. To think that I will, that I desire, that I feel, is, as we have seen, to refer these several forms of consciousness to the thinking subject; or, more properly, to refer willing, desiring, feeling, and thinking all to the same subject "I"; which is related to the latter attribute more especially, merely because the name "I" is given only in and through the recognition of this attribute in the cognition of *cogito*. To infer the existence of the subject from the single attribute of thinking would be to unfold only in part its existence and nature; though it would note that attribute of the subject through the recognition of which in reflection its name was determined and connected with its other attributes.

The latter, namely, our volitions, desires, and feelings, are in general so obscure in respect to the particular causes which precede them and are anterior to their immediate determination or production, that introspective observation in reflection can penetrate only a little way, and is commonly quite unable to trace them back to remote causes in our characters, organizations, and circumstances. Hence, the conception of the causes of our own inward volitions, or our desires and intentions, as being of an inscrutable, non-phenomenal nature, would naturally arise. But this conception would probably be made much more prominent in the unreflective barbarian's mind, by his association of it with the obscurity to him of the inward, or personal, causes of outward actions and expressions in others. Darkness is seen where light is looked for and does not appear. Causes are missed where research is made without success. We are conscious of minds in other men and in other animals only through their outward expressions. The inward causes are not apparent or directly known to us as phenomena; and though the inference of their existence is not in all cases, even with men, made through analogy, or from an observation of their connections with similar outward actions and expressions in ourselves, but is grounded, doubtless, in many cases on go instinctive connection between these expressions in others and *feelings,* at least, in ourselves, yet we do not think of them as really inscrutable m their natures, but only as imperceptible to our outward senses. They have their representatives in the phenomena [p. 244] of our imaginations. These would be but vaguely conceived, however, in many cases. Even reverence in the barbarian's mind might prevent him, as an obedient subject, from attempting to fathom or *reproduce* in his own imagination the thoughts and intentions of his majesty the king. Reverence is not, however, in any case, an unreflective or thoughtless feeling. It would not be like the feelings of the sheep, which, not being able to comprehend through its own experience the savage feelings of the wolf, would only interpret his threatening movements as something fearful, or would connect in an instinctive judgment these outward movements only with anticipated painful consequences. Reverence in the loyal barbarian subject would not go so far as to make his king appear a mere automaton, as the wolf might seem to the sheep. The commands of his king, or of his deity, would be to him rather the voice of a wisdom and authority inscrutable, the outward manifestation of mysterious *power*, the type of metaphysical causation.   Accordingly, we find that a capacity for strong, unappropriated feelings of loyalty and reverence, demanding an object for their satisfaction, have also descended to those thinkers who have inherited "the ontological passion." It would, therefore, appear most probable, that the metaphysician's invincible belief in the conception of the will as a mysterious power behind the inward phenomena of volition, and as incapable of analysis into the determinations of character, organization, and circumstances, arises also from inherited feelings about the wills of other men rather than from attentive observation of the phenomena of his own.

Science and scientific studies have led a portion of the human race a long way aside from the guidance of these inherited intellectual instincts, and have also appeared able to conquer them in many minds to which in youth they seemed invincible. Positivists, unlike poets, become -- are not born -- such thinkers. The conception of the causes of phenomena, with which these studies render them familiar, had small beginnings in the least noble *occupations* and necessities of life, and in the need of knowing the future and judging of it from present signs. From this grew up gradually a knowledge of natural [p. 245] phenomena, and phenomena of mind also, both in their outward and combined orders or laws and in their intimate and elementary successions, or the "laws of nature." The latter are involved in the relation of effects to their "physical" causes, so called because metaphysicians have discovered that they are not the same sort of powers as those which the invincible instincts look for as ultimate and absolute in nature. But this is not a new or modern meaning of the word "cause." It was always its practical, common-sense, every-day meaning; -- in the relations of means to ends; in rational explanations and anticipations of natural events; in the familiar processes and observations of common human life; in short, in the relations of phenomena to phenomena, as apparent causes and effects. This meaning was not well defined, it is true; nor is it now easily made clear, save by examples; yet it is by examples, rather than by a distinct abstraction of what is common to them, that the use of many other words, capable of clear definition, is determined in common language. The relations of invariable succession in phenomena do not, except in ultimate laws where the phenomena are simple or elementary, define the relation of phenomenal cause and effect; for, as it has been observed, night follows day, and day follows night invariably, yet neither is the cause of the other. These relations belong to the *genus* of natural successions. The relation of cause and effect is a *species* of this *genus*. It means an *unconditional* invariable succession; *independence* of other orders of succession, or of all orders not involved in it.

The day illuminates objects; the night obscures them; the sun and fires warm them; the clouds shed rain upon them; the savage animal attacks and hurts others: these facts involve natural orders, in which relations of cause and effect are apparent, and are indicated in the antitheses of their terms as the subjects and objects of transitive propositions. But these relations are only indicated; they are not explicitly set forth. Metaphysics undertakes their explication by referring the illumination, obscurity, warmth, rain and hurt to *powers* in the day, the sun and fires, the clouds, and the animal. Modern metaphysics would not go so far as to maintain, in the light [p. 246] of science, that the powers in these examples are inscrutable, or incapable of further analysis. Nevertheless, when the analysis is made, and the vision of objects, for example, is understood to arise from the incidence of the light of the sun on the air and on objects, and thence from reflections on all surfaces of objects, and thence again from diffused reflections falling partly on our eyes, and so on to the full realization of vision in the brain, all according to determinate laws of succession, -- an analysis which sets forth those *elementary* invariable orders, or *ultimate* and independent laws of succession in phenomena, to which, in their independent combinations, science refers the relations of cause and effect; -- when this analysis has been made, then metaphysics interposes, and, from its ancient habits of thought, ascribes to the elementary antecedent a *power* to produce the elementary consequent. Or when the effect, as in vision, follows from the ultimate properties and elementary laws of great numbers of beings and arrangements, -- the sun, the medium of light, the air, the illuminated objects, the eye, its nerves and the brain, -- and follows through a long series of steps, however rapid, from the earliest to the latest essential antecedent, metaphysics still regards the whole process, with the elementary powers involved, as explicated only in its *outward* features. There is still the mystery inherent in the being of each elementary antecedent, of its power to produce its elementary consequent; and these mysterious powers, combined and referred to the most conspicuous essential conditions of the effect (like the existence of the sun and the eye), make in the whole a mystery as great as if science had never inquired into the process.

Metaphysics demands, in the interest of mystery, why an elementary antecedent is followed by its elementary consequent. But this question does not arise from that inquisitiveness which inspires scientific research. It is asked to show that it cannot be answered, and hence that all science rests on mystery. It is asked from the feelings that in the barbarian or the child forbid or check inquiry. But, being a question, it is open to answer; or it makes legitimate, at least, the counter-question, When can a question be properly [p. 247] asked? or, What is the purpose of asking a question? Is it not to discover the causes, classes, laws, or rules that determine the existence, properties, or production of a thing or event? And when these are discovered, is there any further occasion for inquiry, except in the interest of *feelings* which would have checked inquiry at the outset? The feelings of loyalty and reverence, instinctive in our natures, and of the utmost value in the history of our race, as the mediums of co-operation, discipline, and instruction, are instincts more powerful in some minds than in others, and, like all instincts, demand their proper satisfaction. From the will, or our active powers, they demand devotion; from the intellect, submission to authority and mystery. But, like all instincts, they may demand too much; too much for their proper satisfaction, and even for their most energetic and useful service to the race, or to the individual man. Whether it is possible for any one to have too much loyalty, reverence, love, or devotion, is, therefore, a question which the metaphysical spirit and mode of thought suggest. For in the mystic's mind these feelings have set themselves up as absolute excellencies, as money sets itself up in the mind of the miser. And it is clear that, under these absolute forms, it is difficult to deny the demand. It is only in respect to *what is* reverenced, loved, or worshiped, or *what* claims our allegiance, that questions of how much of them is due can be rationally asked.

To demand the submission of the intellect to the mystery of the simplest and most elementary relations of cause and effect in phenomena, or the restraint of its inquisitiveness on reaching an ultimate law of nature, is asking too much, in that it is a superfluous demand. The intellect in itself has no disposition to go any further, and, on the other hand, no impulse to kneel before its completed triumph. The highest generality, or universality, in the elements or connections of elements in phenomena, is the utmost reach both in the power and the desire of the scientific intellect. Explanation cannot go, and does not rationally seek to go, beyond such facts. The invention of *noumena* to account for ultimate and universal properties and relations in phenomena arises from no other necessity [p. 248] than the action of a desire urged beyond the normal promptings of its power. To demand of the scientific intellect that it shall pause in the interest of mystery at the movements of a falling body or at the laws of these movements, is a misappropriation of the quality of mystery. For mystery still has its uses; and, in its useful action, is an ally of inquisitiveness, in citing and guiding it, giving it steadiness and seriousness, opposing only its waywardness and idleness. It fixes attention, even inquisitive attention, on its objects, and in its active form of wonder "is a highly philosophical affection." So also devotion, independently of its intrinsic worth in the mystic's regard, has its uses; and these determine its rational measure, or how much of it is due to any object. In its active forms of usefulness and duty, it is an ally of freedom in action, opposing this freedom only in respect to what would limit it still more, or injuriously and on the whole.

The metaphysical modes of thought and feeling foster, on the other hand, the sentiments of mystery and devotion in their passive forms, and as attitudes of the intellect and will, rather than as their inciting and guiding motives. These attitudes, which are symbolized in the forms of religious worship, were no doubt needed to fix the attention of the barbarian, as they are still required to fix the attention of the child upon serious contemplations and purposes. Obedience and absolute submission are, at one stage of intellectual and moral development, both in a race and in the individual, required as the conditions of discipline for effecting the more directly serviceable and freer action of the mind and character under the guidance of rational loyalty and reverence. The metaphysical modes of thought and feeling retain these early habits in relations in which they have ceased to be serviceable to the race, or to the useful development of the individual, especially when in the mystic's regard obedience has acquired an intrinsic worth, and submission has become a beatitude. The scientific habit of thought, though emancipated from any such outward supports and constraints, is yet not wanting in earnestness of purpose and serious interests, and is not without the motives of devotion and mystery, or their active guidance in the directions of usefulness [p. 249] and duty, and in the investigations of truth. It does not stand in awe before the unknown, as if life itself depended on a mysterious and capricious will in that unknown; for awe is habitual only with the barbarian, and is a useful motive only in that severe instruction which is exacted by the wants, insecurities, and necessities of his life, while among the partially civilized it often constrains the thoughtless by a present fear to avoid or resist evils really greater than what is feared, though less obvious to the imagination.

Nevertheless, the whole nature of the modern civilized man includes both these opposing tendencies in speculation, the metaphysical and scientific; the disposition to regard the phenomena of nature as they appeared naturally and serviceably in the primitive use of language and reflection, and the disposition of the Positivist to a wholly different interpretation of them. A conflict between them arises, however, only where either disposition invades the proper province of the other; where both strive for supremacy in the search for a clearer knowledge of these phenomena, or where both aim to satisfy the more primitive and instinctive tendencies of the mind. In the forms of ontological and phenomenological, or metaphysical and positive philosophies, this conflict is unavoidable and endless. Deathless warriors, irreconcilable and alternately victorious, according to the nature of the ground, or to advantages of position, continually renew their struggles along the line of development in each individual mind and character. A contrast of tendencies analogous to this, which involves, however, no necessary conflict, is shown in the opposition of science and poetry; the one contemplating in understanding and in fixed positive beliefs the phenomena which the other contemplates through firmly established and instinctive tendencies, and through interests, which for want of a better name to note their motive power, or influence in the will, are also sometimes called beliefs. Disputes about the nature of what is called "belief," as to what it is, as well as to what are the true grounds or causes of it, would, if the meanings of the word were better discriminated in common usage, be settled by the lexicographer; for it is really an ambiguous term. Convictions of half-truths, or intimations [p. 250] of truth, coupled with deep feeling, and impressed by the rhythms and alliterations of words, are obviously different from those connections which logic and evidence are calculated to establish in the mind.

The poet inherits in his mental and moral nature, or organic memory, and in his dispositions of feeling and imagination, the instinctive thoughts and feelings which we have supposed habitual and useful in the outward life of the barbarian. In the melody of his verses he revives the habits which were acquired, it is believed, in the development of his race, long before any words were spoken, or were needed to express its imaginations, and when its emotions found utterance in the music of inarticulate tones. The poet's productions are thus, in part, reproductions, refined or combined in the attractive forms of art, of what was felt and thought before language and science existed; or they are restorations of language to a primeval use, and to periods in the history of his race in which his progenitors uttered their feelings, as of gallantry, defiance, joy, grief, exultation, sorrow, fear, anger, or love, and gave expression to their light, serious, or violent moods, in modulated tones, harsh or musical; or later, in unconscious figures of speech, expressed without reflection or intention of communicating truth. For, as it has been said, it is essential to eloquence to be heard, but poetry is expression to be only overheard. In supposing this noble savage ancestry for the poet, and for those who overhear in him, with a strange delight and interest, a charm of naturalness and of novelty combined by the magic of his art, it is not necessary to conclude that all savage natures are noble, or have in them the germs of the poet's inspiration. It is more probable that most of the races which have remained in a savage state have retained a more primitive condition, in many respects, than that of civilized men, because they lacked some qualities possessed by the *noble* savage which have advanced him to the civilized state, and because they have been isolated from the effects of such qualities either to improve or exterminate them. The noble savage is not, at any rate, now to be found. Weeding out the more stupid and brutal varieties has, doubtless, been the effective method of nature in the culture of the nobler qualities [p. 251] of men, at least in that state of nature which was one of warfare.

It is a common misconception of the theory of evolution to suppose that any one of contemporary races, or species derived from a common origin, fully represents   the characters of its progenitors, or that they are not all more or less divergent forms of an original race; the ape, for example, as well as the man, from a more remote stock, or the present savage man, as well as the civilized one, from a more recent common origin. Original differences within a race are, indeed, the conditions of such divergences, or separations of a race into several; and original superiorities, though slight at first and accidental, were thus the conditions of the survival of those who possessed them, and of tie extinction of others from their struggles in warfare, in gallantry, and for subsistence. The secondary distinctions of sex, or contrasts in the personal attractions, in the forms, movements, aspects, voices, and even in some mental dispositions of men and women, are, on the whole, greatest ill the races which have accomplished most, not merely in science and the useful arts, but more especially in the arts of sculpture, painting, music, and poetry. And this in the theory of evolution is not an accidental conjunction, but a connection through a common origin. Love is still the theme of poets, and his words are measured by laws of rhythm, which in a primeval race served in vocal music, with other charms, to allure in the contests of gallantry. There would, doubtless, have arisen from these rivalries a sort of self-attention[8] for an outward self-consciousness, which, together with the consciousness of themselves as causes distinct from the wills or agencies of other beings, and as having feelings, or passive powers, and desires, or latent volitions, not shared by others, served in the case of the primitive men as bases of reference in their first attention to the phenomena of thought in their minds, when these became sufficiently vivid to engage attention in the revival of trains of images through acts of reflection. The consummate self-consciousness, expressed by "I think," needed for its genesis only the power of attending to the phenomena of thought as signs of other thoughts, or of images revived from memory, with a reference of them to a subject; that is, to a something possessing other attributes, or to a group of co-existent phenomena. The most distinct attention to this being, or subject, of volitions, desires, feelings, outward expressions, and thoughts required a name for the subject, as other names were required for the most distinct attention to the several phenomena themselves.

This view of the origin of self-consciousness is by no means necessarily involved in the much more certain and clearly apparent agency of natural selection in the process of development. For natural selection is not essentially concerned in the *first* production of any form, structure, power, or habit, but only in perpetuating and improving those which have arisen from any cause whatever. its agency is the same in preserving and increasing a serviceable and heritable feature in any form of life, whether this service be incidental to some other already existing and useful power which is turned to account in some new direction, or be the unique and isolated service of some newly and arbitrarily implanted nature. Whether the powers of memory and abstractive attention, already existing and useful in outward perceptions common to men and others of the more intelligent animals, were capable in their higher degrees and under favorable circumstances (such as the gestural and vocal powers of primeval man afforded them) of being turned to a new service in the power of reflection, aided by language, or were supplemented by a really new, unique, and inexplicable power, in either case, the agency of natural selection would have been the same in preserving, and also in improving, the new faculty, provided this faculty was capable of improvement by degrees, and was not perfect from the first. The origin of that which through service to life has been preserved, is to this process arbitrary, indifferent, accidental (in the logical sense of this word), or non-essential. This origin has no part in the process, and is of importance with reference to it only in determining how much it has to do to complete the work of creation. For if a faculty has small beginnings, and rises to great [p. 253] importance in the development of a race through natural selection, then the process becomes an essential one. But if men were put in possession of the faculties which so pre-eminently distinguish them by a sudden, discontinuous, arbitrary cause or action, or without reference to what they were before, except so far as their former faculties were adapted to the service of the new ones, then selection might only act to preserve or maintain at their highest level faculties so implanted. Even the effects of constant, direct us~, habit, or long-continued exercise might be sufficient to account for all improvements in a faculty. The latter means of improvement must, indeed, on either hypothesis, have been very influential in increasing the range of the old powers of memory, attention, and vocal utterance through their new use.

The outward physical aids of reflective thought, in the articulating powers of the voice, do not appear to have been firmly implanted, with the new faculty of self-consciousness, among the instincts of human nature; and this, at first sight, might seem to afford an argument against the acquisition by a natural process of any form of instinct, since vocal language has probably existed as long as any useful or effective exercise of reflection in men. That the faculty which uses the voice in language should be inherited, while its chief instrument is still the result of external training in an art, or that language should be "half instinct and half art," would, indeed, on second thought, be a paradox on any other hypothesis but that of natural selection. But this is an economical process, and effects no more than what is needed. If the instinctive part in language is sufficient to prompt the invention and the exercise of the art,[9] then the inheritance of instinctive powers of articulation would be superfluous, and would not be effected by selection; but would only come in the form of inherited effects of habit, -- the form in which the different degrees of aptitude for the education of the voice appear to exist in different races of men. Natural selection would not effect anything, indeed, [p. 254] for men which art and intelligence could, and really do, effect, -- such as clothing their backs in cold climates with hair or fur, -- since this would be quite superfluous under the furs of other animals with which art has already clothed them. The more instinctive language of gestures appears also to have only indirect relations to real serviceableness, or to the grounds of natural selection, and to depend on the inherited effects of habit, and on universal principles of mental and physiological action. [10]

The language of gestures may, however, have been sufficient for the realization of the faculty of self-consciousness In all that the metaphysician regards as essential to it. The primitive man might, by pointing to himself in a meditative attitude, have expressed in effect to himself and others the "I think," which was to be, in the regard of many of his remote descendants, the distinguishing mark, the outward emblem, of his essential separation from his nearest kindred and progenitors, of his metaphysical distinction from all other animals. This consciousness and expression would more naturally have been a source of proud satisfaction to the primitive men themselves, just as children among us glory most in their first imperfect command of their unfolding powers, or even in accomplishments of a unique and individual character when first acquired. To the civilized man of the present time, there is more to be proud of in the immeasurable consequences of this faculty, and in what was evolved through the continued subsequent exercise of it, especially through its outward artificial instruments in language, -- consequences not involved in the bare faculty itself As being the pre-requisite condition of these uses and inventions, it would, if of an ultimate and underived nature, be worthy the distinction, which, in case it is referable to latent natures in pre-existing faculties; must be accorded to them in their higher degrees. And if these faculties are common to all the more intelligent animals, and are, by superior degrees only, made capable of higher functions, or effects of a new and different kind (as longer fins enable a fish to fly), then the main qualitative distinction of the human race is to be sought for in [p. 255] these effects, and chiefly in the invention and use of artificial language.

This invention was, doubtless, at first made by men from social motives, for the purpose of making known to one another, by means of arbitrarily associated and voluntary signs, the wishes, thoughts, or intentions clearly determined upon in their imaginations. Even now, children invent words, or, rather, attribute meanings to the sounds they can command, when they are unable to enunciate the words of the mother tongue which they desire for the purposes of communication. It is, perhaps, improper to speak of this stage of language as determined by conscious invention through a recognized motive, and for a *purpose* in the subjective sense of this word. It is enough for a purpose (in its objective sense) to be served, or for a service to be done, by such arbitrary associations between internal and external language, or thought and speech, however these ties may, in the first instance, be brought about. The intention and the invention become, however, conscious acts in reflection when the secondary motives to the use of language begin to exert influence, and perhaps before the latter have begun to be reflectively known, or recognized, and while they are still acting as they would in a merely animal mind. These motives are the needs and desires (or, rather, the use and importance), of making our thoughts clearer to ourselves, and not merely of communicating them to others. Uncertainty, or perplexity from failures of memory or understanding, render the mnemonic uses of vivid external and voluntary signs the agents of important services to reflective thought, when these signs are already possessed, to some extent, for the purposes of communication. These two uses of language, -- the social, and the meditative or mnemonic, -- carried to only a slight development, would afford the means of recognizing their own values, as well as the character of the inventions of which languages would be seen to consist. Invention in its true sense, as a reflective process, would then act with more energy in extending the range of language.

Command of language is a much more efficient command of thought in reflective processes than that which is implied in [p. 256] the simplest form of self-consciousness. It involves a command of memory to a certain degree. Already a mental power, usually accounted a simple one, and certainly not involved in "I think," or only in its outward consequences, has been developed in the power of the will over thought. Voluntary memory, or reminiscence, is especially aided by command of language. This is a tentative process, essentially similar to that of a search for a lost or missing external object. Trials are made in it to revive a missing mental image, or train of images, by means of words; and, on the other hand, to revive a missing name by means of mental images, or even by other words. It is not certain that this power is an exclusively human one, as is generally believed, except in respect to the high degree of proficiency attained by men in its use. It does not appear impossible that an intelligent dog may be aided by its attention, purposely directed to spontaneous memories, in recalling a missing fact, such as the locality of a buried bone.

In the earlier developments of language, and while it is still most subject to the caprices and facilities of individual wills (as in the nursery), the character of it as an invention, or system of inventions, is, doubtless, more clearly apparent than it afterwards becomes, when a third function of language rises into prominence. Traditions, by means of language, and customs, fixed by its conservative power, tend, in turn, to give fixity to the conventions of speech; and the customs and associations of language itself begin to prescribe rules for its inventions, or to set limits to their arbitrary adoption. Individual wills lose their power to decree changes in language; and, indeed, at no time are individual wills unlimited agents in this process. Consent given on grounds not always consciously determining it, but common to the many minds which adopt proposals or obey decrees in the inventions of words, is always essential to the establishment or alteration of a language. But as soon as a language has become too extensive to be the possible invention of any single mind, and is mainly a tradition, it must appear to the barbarian's imagination to have a will of its own; or, rather, sounds and meanings must appear naturally bound together, [p. 257]and to be the fixed names and expressions of wills in things. And later, then complex grammatical forms and abstract substantive names have found their way into languages, they must appear like the very laws and properties of nature itself, which nothing but magical powers could alter; though magic, with its power over the will, might still be equal to the miracle. Without this power not even a sovereign's will could oppose the authority of language in its own domain. Even magic had failed when an emperor could not alter the gender of a noun. Education had become the imperial power, and schoolmasters were its prime ministers.

From this point in the development of language, its separations into the *varieties* of dialects, the divergences of these into *species*, or distinct languages, and the affinities of them as grouped by the glossologist into *genera* of languages, present precise parallels to the developments and relations in the organic world which the theory of natural selection supposes. It has been objected[11] to the completeness of these parallels that the process of development in languages is still under the control of men's wills. Though an individual will may have but little influence on it, yet the general consent to a proposed change is still a voluntary action, or is composed of voluntary actions on the part of the many, and hence is essentially different from the choice in natural selection, when acting within its proper province. To this objection it may be replied, that a general consent to a change, or even an assent to the reasons for it, does not really constitute a voluntary act in respect to the whole language itself; since it does not involve in itself any intention on the part of the many to change the language. Moreover, the conscious intention of effecting a change on the part of the individual author, or speaker, is not the agent by which the change is effected; or is only an incidental cause, no more essential to the process than the causes which produce variations are to the process of natural selection in species. Let the causes of variation be what they may, -- miracles even, -- yet all the conditions of selection are fulfilled, provided the variations [p. 258] can be developed by selection, or will more readily occur in the selected successors of the forms in which they first appear in useful degrees. These conditions do not include the prime causes of variations, but only the causes which facilitate their action through inheritance, and ultimately make it normal or regular.

So, also, the reasons or motives which in general are not consciously perceived, recognized, or assented to, but none the less determine the consent of the many to changes in language, are the real causes of the selection, or the choice of usages in words. Let the cause of a *proposed* change in language be what it may -- an act of free will, a caprice, or inspiration even -- provided there is something in the proposition calculated to gain the consent of the many, -- such as ease of enunciation, the authority of an influential speaker or writer, distinctness from other words already appropriated to other meanings, the influence of vague analogies in relations of sound and sense (accidental at first, but tending to establish fixed roots in etymology or even to create instinctive connections of sound and sense), -- such motives or reasons, common to the many, and not their consenting wills, are the causes of choice and change in the usages of speech. Moreover, these motives are not usually recognized by the many, but act instinctively. Hence, there is no intention in the many, either individually or collectively, to change even a single usage, -- much less a whole language. The laws or constitution of the language, as it exists, appear, even to the reflecting few, to be unchanged; and the proposed change appears to be justified by these laws, as corrections or extensions of previous usages.

The case is parallel to the developments of legal usages, or principles of judicial decisions. The judge cannot rightfully change the laws that govern his judgments; and the just judge does not consciously do so. Nevertheless, legal usages change from age to age. Laws, in their practical effects, are ameliorated by courts as well as by legislatures. No new principles are consciously introduced; but interpretations of old ones, and combinations, under more precise and qualified statements, are made, which disregard old decisions, seemingly by [p. 259] new and better definitions of that which in its nature is unalterable, but really, in their practical effects, by alterations, at least in the proximate grounds of decision; so that nothing is really unalterable in law, except the intention to do justice under universally applicable principles of decision, and the instinctive judgments of so-called natural law.

In like manner, there is nothing unalterable in the traditions of a language, except the instinctive motives to its acquisition and use, and some instinctive connections of sense and sound. *Intention* -- so far as it is operative in the many who determine what a language is, or what is proper to any language -- is chiefly concerned in *not* changing it; that is, in conforming to what is regarded by them as established usage. That usages come in under the form of good and established ones, while in fact they are new though good inventions, is not due to the intention of the speakers who adopt them. The intention of those who consciously adopt new forms or meanings in words is to conform to what appears legitimate; or it is to fill out or improve usages in accordance with existing analogies, and not to alter the essential features in a language. But unconsciously they are also governed by tendencies in themselves and others, -- vague feelings of fitness and other grounds of choice which are outside of the actual traditions of speech; and, though a choice may be made in their minds between an old and a really new usage, it is commonly meant as a truly conservative choice, and from the intention of not altering the language in its essence, or not following what is regarded as a deviation from correct usage. The actual and continuous changes, completely transforming languages, which their history shows, are not, then, due to the intentions of those who speak, or have spoken, them, and cannot, in any sense, be attributed to the agency of their wills, if, as is commonly the case, their intentions are just the reverse. For the same wills cannot act from contradictory intentions, both to conserve and to change a language on the whole.

It becomes an interesting question, therefore, when in general anything can be properly said to be effected by the will of man. Man is an agent in producing many effects, both in nature and [p. 260] in himself, which appear to have no different general character from that of effects produced by other animals, even the lowest in the animal series, or by plants, or even by inorganic forces. Man, by transporting and depositing materials, in making, for example, the shell-mounds of the stone age, or the works of modern architecture and engineering, or in commerce and agriculture, is a geological agent; like the polyps which build the coral reefs, and lay the foundations of islands, or make extensions to mainlands; or like the vegetation from which the ; coal-beds were deposited; or like winds, rains, rivers, and the currents of the ocean; and his agency is not in any way different in its general character, and with reference to its geological effects from that of unconscious beings. In relation to these effects his agency is, in fact, unconscious, or at least *unintended.*

Moreover, in regard to interval effects, the modification of his own mind and character by influences external to himself, under which he comes accidentally, and without intention; many effects upon his emotions and sentiments from impressive incidents, or the general surroundings of the life with which he has become associated through his own agency, -- these, as unintended effects, are the same in general character, as if his own agency had not been concerned in them, -- as if he had been without choice in his pursuits and surroundings.

Mingled with these unintended effects upon himself, there are, of course, others, either actually or virtually intended, and, I therefore, his own effects. If, for example, in conformity with surrounding fashions of dress, he should choose to clothe himself, and should select some one from the existing varieties in these fashions, or should even add, *consciously*, a new feature to them from his individual taste in dress, in each case he would be acting from intention, and the choice would be his own. But so far as he has thus affected the proportions among these varieties, or tends further to affect them by his example, the action is not his own volition, unless we include *within* the will's agency what is properly said to act either *through* or *upon* the will; namely, that which, by an undistinguished influence, I guides taste and choice in himself and the others who follow unconsciously his example. Those influences of example and [p. 261] instinctive, or even educated, tastes, which are not raised by distinct attention into conscious motives, would not be allowed by the metaphysician to be parts in the will's action. It would not be *within* but *through* its action that these influences would produce their unintended effects. According to the less definite and precise *physical* theory of the will's action, these effects might be regarded as voluntary; but then the choice would not be different in its character from that effected through other kinds of physical agency. On neither theory, therefore, can unintended effects, or the effects of unrecognized causes acting through the will, be regarded as different in their character from the general results of selection in nature. On the physical theory of the will, man's agency is merged in ·that of nature generally; but according to the metaphysician's more definite understanding of voluntary actions, which is also that of common usage, *intention* would appear to be the mark by which to determine whether anything is the effect of the will of man, except in an accidental or non-essential manner.

An apparently serious objection to this test arises, however, in reference to another mark of voluntary action, and of the efficacy of the will. The mark *of responsibility* (the subject of moral or legal discipline, the liability to blame or punishment) is justly regarded as the mark of free human agency. But the limits set by this mark are beyond what is actually *intended* in our actions. We are often held responsible, and properly, for more than we intend, or for what we *ought* to have intended. The absence of intention (namely, of the intention of doing differently) renders us liable to blame, when it is involved in the absence of the more general intention of doing right, or of doing what the discipline of responsibility has commanded or implied in its commands. Carelessness, or want of forethought, cannot be said to involve intention in any case, but in many cases it is blameworthy or punishable; since in such cases moral discipline presupposes or presumes intention, or else seeks, as in the case of children, by punishment to turn attention upon moral principles, and upon what is implied in them, whether set forth in instincts, examples, precepts, or commandments. But this extension of the sphere of personal [p. 262] agency and accountability to relations in which effects upon will and character are sought to be produced by moral and legal discipline, its extension beyond what the will itself produces in its direct action, has nothing to do with strictly scientific or theoretical inquiries concerning effects, in which neither the foreseeing nor the obedient will can be an agent or factor, but of which the intellect is rather the recorder, or mere accountant.

If the question concerning the origin of languages were, Who are responsible for their existence and progressive changes, or ought to be credited for improvements, or blamed for deficiencies[*sic*] in them? or if the question were, How men might -- or should be made better inventors, or apter followers of the best inventions, -- there would then be some pertinency in insisting on the agency of man in their developments, -- an agency which, in fact, like his agency in geology, is incidental to his real volitions, and is neither involved in what he intends nor in what he could be made to intend by discipline. So far as human intentions have had anything to do with changes in the traditions of language, they have, as we have said, been exerted in resisting them. Hence the traditions of language, with all the knowledge, histories, arts, and sciences involved and embodied in them, are developments incidental, it is true, to the existence and exercise of self-consciousness, and of free or intelligent wills, yet are developments around and outside of them, so to speak, and were added to them rather than evolved from them. These developments were added through their exercise and serviceableness as powers which stand to the more primitive ones of self-conscious thought and volition in relations similar to those we have seen to exist between the latter and the still more primitive powers of mind in memory and attention.

These relations come, first, from turning an old power to a new account; or making a new use of it, when the power, developed for other uses, acquires the requisite energy (as when the fins of a fish become fitted for flying); or when the revivals of memory become vivid enough to make connecting thoughts in a train distinct and apparent as mere signs to a [p. 263] reflective attention. Secondly, the new use increases the old power by its exercise and serviceableness (as flying and its value to life make the fins of the fish still longer), or as the exercise and importance to life of reflective thought make the revivals of memory still more vivid, and enlarge its organ, the brain. Traditions of language, or established artifices of expression, are related to new uses in a power, now in turn become sufficiently energetic, which at first was only the power of associating the sounds of words with thoughts, and thence with their objects, and which was incidental to the distinct recognition of thoughts as signs, or suggestions, of other thoughts. Developed by exercise and its serviceableness to life to the point, not only of making readily and employing temporarily such arbitrary associations, but also of fixing them and transmitting them as a more or less permanent language, or system of signs, this power acquired, or was turned to, a use involving immeasurable consequences and values.

To choose arbitrarily for preservation and transmission one out of many arbitrary associations of sounds with a meaning could not have been a rational or intelligent act of free will, but ought rather to be attributed to chance, lot, or fate; or to *will* in the narrower sense of the word in which one man is said to have more than another, or to be more willful, that is, persistent in his caprices. To make by decree any action permanent and regular which in itself is transient or accidental requires *will* it is true, in one sense, or *sticking to a point, merely because if has been assumed*; as some children do in imposing their inventions upon their associates. This degree *of arbitrariness* appears necessary to the step in the use of signs which made them traditions of language, permanent enough to be the roots of a continued growth in it, -- a growth which must, however, have determined more and more the selections of new words, and new uses in old ones, through motives common to the many speakers of a language; such as common fancies, instinctive tendencies, facilities, allegiance to authority, and associations in general-the vague as well as distinct ones -- which were common to many speakers. These causes would act instinctively, or unconsciously, as well [p. 264] as by design. Tyranny in the growth of language, or the agency of arbitrary wills, persisting in their caprices, must have disappeared at an early date, or must have become insignificant in its effects upon the whole of any established language. Intentional choice would henceforward have the *design* generally of conserving or restoring a supposed good usage; though along with unintended preferences, instinctively followed, it would, doubtless, have the effect of slowly changing the usages of language on the whole. A happy suggestion of change would be adopted, if adopted consciously, with reference to its supposed conformity to *the genius* of the language, or to its will, rather than to the will of an individual dictator; and the influence of a speaker would depend on the supposition that he knew best how to use the language correctly, or was intimate with its genius. But suggestions of change would be more likely to be adopted unconsciously.

History can trace languages back only, of course, to the earliest times of their representations in phonetic writings or inscriptions; as palæontology can trace organic species back only to the earliest preservation of them as fossils in the rocks. In neither case do we probably go back to periods in which forms were subject to sudden or capricious variations.

Natural selection would, therefore, define the most prominent action of the causes of change in both of them. But just as governments in all their forms depend on the fixedness and force of traditions, and as traditions gained this force through the wills of those in the past who established them by arbitrary decrees, and induced in others those habits of respect and obedience which now preserve them, so in language there was, doubtless, a time when *will* was the chief agent in its formation and preservation. But it was Will in its narrower sense, which does not include all that is commonly meant by volitional action. The latter involves, it is true, persistence in some elements, -- a persistence in memory and thought of consciously recognized motives, principles, purposes, or intentions. Volition is an action through memory, and not merely from a present stimulus, and is accompanied, when free or *rational,* by the recognition in thought of the motive, the proximate cause of the action, [p. 265] the reasons for it, or the immediate and present tendency to it, which is referred back in turn, but is not analyzed, nor usually capable of being analyzed introspectively into still more remote antecedents in our histories, inherited disposition, characters, and present circumstances. Those causes which are even too feeble to be introspectively recognized are not, of course, the source whence the force or energy of will is derived; but independently of their *directive* agency, this force is indistinguishable from that of pure spontaneity or vital energy. In like manner, the force of water in a system of river-courses is not determined by its beds and banks, but is none the less guided by them. This water-force in the first instance, and from time to time, alters its courses, but normally flows within predetermined courses; as the energy of will flows normally within the directive, but alterable, courses of character and circumstances. The really recognized motives in ordinary volition generally include more than the impulse or satisfaction of adhering to an assumed position, or to a purpose, for the will's sake, as in mere will, or willfulness which is an overflow, so to speak, of energy, directed only by its own inertia, though often useful in altering character, or the courses of volition, both in the will itself and the wills of others. The habit of conscious persistence, involved in will, but most conspicuous in self-will, was, together with its correlatives, respect and obedience, doubtless serviceable to the rulers of primeval men, the authors of human government; and was, doubtless, developed through this serviceableness before it was turned to new uses in the institution of arbitrary customs and traditions. It thus illustrates anew the general principle shown ill the several previous steps *of* this progress, namely, the turning of an old power to a new account, or making a new use of it, when the power has acquired the requisite energy; and the subsequent further increase of the power through serviceableness and exercise in its new function.

This power in the wills of the political, military, and religious leaders of men must soon, after producing the apotheosis of the more influential among them, have been converted into the sacred force of tradition; that is, into the *fas* or commands [p. 266] of languages themselves; and of other arbitrary customs. Henceforth and throughout all the periods included in the researches of comparative philology in which written remains of languages are to be found, it is probable that no man has consciously committed, or had the power to commit, the sin of intentionally altering their traditions, except for reasons common to many speakers and afforded by the traditions themselves.

Footnotes

[1] For an intellect complete without appendages of sense or locomotion, see Plato's Timæus, 33, 34.·

[2] It appears, at first sight, a rash hypothesis to imagine so extensive an action of illusion as I have supposed in the revivals of memory,-- a self-vouching faculty of which, in general, the testimony cannot be questioned,-since each recall asserts for itself in identity with what is recalled by it, either in past outward experiences or in previous revivals of them. Eat the hypothesis of uniform, or frequent, illusions in individual judgments of memory is not made in contradiction of experiences in general, including those remembered, when reduced to rational consistency. The familiar fact that no memory, even of an immediately past experience, is an adequate reproduction of everything that must have been present in it in   actual

consciousness, and must have received more or less attention, is familiarly verified by repeating the remembered experience. Memory itself thus testifies to its own fallibility. But this is not all. Illusion in an opposite direction, the more than adequate revival of some experiences, so far as vividness and apparently remembered details are concerned, affects our memories of dreams, demonstrably in some, presumably in many. What is commonly called a dream is not what is present to the imagination in sleep, but what is believed, often illusively, to have been present; and is, doubtless, in general, more vivid in memory and furnished with more numerous details, owing to the livelier action of imagination in waking moments. The liveliness of an actual dream is rather in its dominant feeling or interest than in its images.

The order of internal events, or the order of suggestion in actual dreams, is often reversed in the waking memories of them. A dream very long and full of details, as it appears in memory, and taking many words to relate, is sometimes recalled from the suggestions and trains of thought in sleep which are comprised in the impressions of a few moments. Such a dream usually ends in some startling or interesting event, which was a misinterpretation in sleep of some real outward impression, as a loud or unusual noise, or some inward sensation, like one of hunger, thirst, heat, cold, or numbness, which really stood in sleep at the beginning of the misremembered train of thought, instead or constituting its *dénouement* in a remembered series of real incidents. The remembered dream *seems* to have been an isolated series of such incidents, succeeding each other in the natural order of experience; but this appearance may well arise from the absence of any remembered indications of a contrary order; or from the absence, on one hand, of a consciousness in sleep of anything more vivid than the actual dream, and the real feebleness, on the other hand, of the dream itself in respect to everything in it except the salient incident, or the dominant interest, which caused it to be remembered along with the feeble sketch of suggested incidents. Surprise at incongruities in parts of trains often constitutes this interest.

If the waking imagination really fills out this sketch, and avouches the whole without cheek from anything really remembered, the phenomenon would be perfectly accordant with what is known of the dealings of imagination with real experiences, and with what is to be presumed of the comparative feebleness of its powers in sleep. A remembered dream would thus be, in some cases, a twofold illusion,--an illusion in sleep arising from misinterpreted sensations, and an illusion in memory concerning what was actually the train of thoughts excited by the mistake, the train being in fact often inverted in such an apparent recollection. Savages and the insane believe their dreams to be real experiences. The civilized and sane man believes them to be true memories of illusions in sleep. A step farther in the application of the general tests of true experience would reduce some dreams to illusive memories of the illusions of sleep.

There does not appear on analysis, made in conformity to the reality of experiences in general, that there is any intrinsic difference between a memory and an imagination, the reality of the former being dependent on extrinsic relations, and the outward checks of other memories. Memory, as a whole, vouches for itself, and for all its mutually consistent details, and banishes mere imaginations from its province, not as foreigners, but on account of their lawlessness, or incoherence with the rest of its subjects, and it does so through the exercise of what is called the judgments of experience, which are in fact mnemonic summaries of experiences (including instinctive tendencies). The imaginations of the insane are in insurrection against this authority of memory in general experience, or against what is familiarly called "reason." When sufficiently vivid, or powerful, and numerous, they usurp the powers of state, or the authority of memory and free intelligent volition. "Reason" is then said to be "dethroned."

The unreality of some dreams would thus appear to be more complete than they are in general discovered to be by mature, sane, and reflective thought, and by indirect observations upon their conditions and phenomena. The supposition of a similar illusion in the phenomena of reflection on the immediately past, or passing, impressions of the mind affords an explanation of a curious phenomenon, not uncommon in waking moments, which is referred to by many writers on psychology, namely, the phenomenon of experiencing in minute detail what appears also to be recalled as a past experience. Some writers have attempted to explain this as a veritable revival, by a passing experience, of a really past and very remote one, either in our progenitors, as some evolutionists suppose; or in a previous life, or in some state of individual existence, otherwise unremembered, as the mystic prefers to believe: a revival affected by an actual coincidence, in many minute particulars, of a present real experience with a really past one. But if a passing real experience could be supposed to be divided, so to speak, or to make a double impression in memory, -- one the ordinary impression of what is immediately past, and the other a dream-like impression filled out on its immediate revival in reflection with the same derails, -- the supposition would be in accordance with what is really known of some dreams, and would, therefore, be more probable than the above explanations. It is possible to trust individual memories too far, even in respect to what is immediately past, as it is to trust too far a single sense in respect to what is immediately present. Rational consistency, in all experiences, or in experience on the whole, is the ultimate test of reality or truth in our judgments, whether these *are* "intuitive." or consciously derived.

[3]Images in dogs are supposed to depend largely on the sense of smell.

[4] Dr. McCosh, On the Intuitions of the Mind, etc.

[5] See Mill's Logic, Book II., chapter iii.

[6] See Mill's Examination of Hamilton, chapter xi.

[7] See Mill's Examination or Hamilton, chapter v.

[8] See Darwin's Expression of the Emotions in Men and Animals. Theory of Blushing, chapter xiii.

[9] In the origin of the languages of civilized peoples. the distinction between powers of tradition, or *external inheritance*, and proper invention in art becomes a very important one, as will be shown farther on.

[10] See Darwin's Expression of the Emotions in Man and Animals.

[11] See article on Schleicher and the Physical Theory of Language, in Professor W. D. Whitney's Oriental and Linguistic Studies.